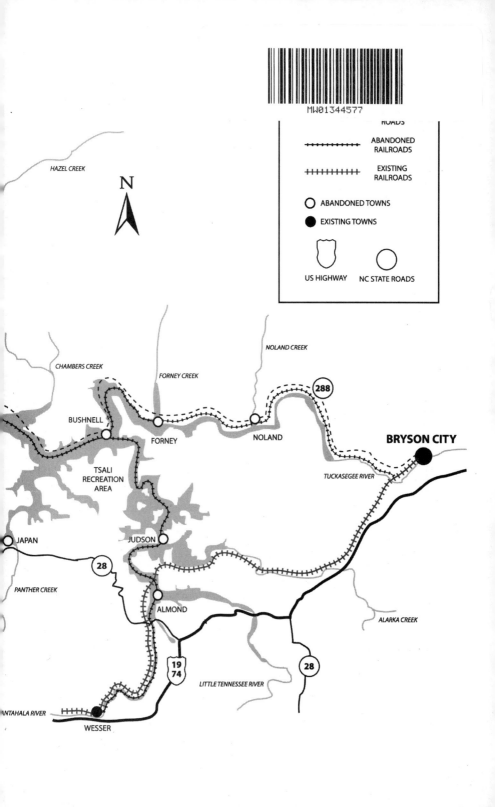

# Fontana

## A Pocket History of Appalachia

BY LANCE HOLLAND

©2001 by Lance Holland
All rights reserved

ISBN 0-9664720-1-2
Library of Congress Control Number 2001088813

Appalachian History Series
1241 Lower Stecoah Road
Robbinsville, NC 28771
www.appalachianhistoryseries.com

Editing by George Ellison and Duane Oliver
Book design and production by Ron Roman/Treehouse Communications
www.treehousecomm.com

Printed in the United States

This book is sold with the understanding that the author and publisher assume no legal responsibility for the completeness or accuracy of the contents of this book, nor for any damages incurred while attempting to visit any locations described within it. The text is based on information available at the time of publication.

## PREFACE

A study of the cultural and natural history of any given geographical area of land can be related to other similar geographical areas. The particular area under study could be called a pocket of land. Certain similarities in the evolution and development of these comparable areas, particularly when in the same general region, can offer insights into the history of the larger area. The cultural and natural history of the geographical area affected by the construction of Fontana Dam and Lake is representative of the gamut of changes that occurred throughout the mountains of the southern United States. A study of the places, people, and events relating to this area of western North Carolina will reveal a historic picture that is representative of the history of all the Appalachians. Michner's study of the fictitious *Centennial* provided an overview of the settlement of the American West. Hopefully, *Fontana* will do the same for the southern Appalachians—but it is the real history of a real place.

## ACKNOWLEDGMENTS

The completion of this book would not have been a reality without the help and encouragement of many people. Although I am sure I have inadvertently omitted someone, a list of these people is under the heading "Interviews and Contributions" in the Sources of Information section at the end of the book. Several people deserve special thanks for their invaluable help with the actual production of the work: Tina Holland, my wife, for her endless hours of help in collecting the material, typing, and checking the manuscript; Heather Holland, my daughter, for encouragement and support; George Ellison and Duane Oliver—my editors, fellow historians, and friends; and Ron Roman, the designer who took the manuscript and the photographs and made this pretty book out of them.

A sincere thank you,
Lance Holland
Stecoah, North Carolina

# Contents

HOLLAND COLLECTION

Chapter 1— Page 9
**THE ORIGINAL PEOPLE**
Early Indians; The Cherokee; Nikwasi; Trail of Tears; Tsali.

Chapter 2— Page 23
**THE FIRST EUROPEANS**
Early Traders; Sir Alexander Cumming; Fort Loudon; William Bartram.

Chapter 3— Page 33
**SETTLERS TRICKLE IN**
Moses and Patience Proctor; Jesse and Catherine Gunter.

Chapter 4— Page 45
**SUBTERRANEAN SMOKIES**
Fonzie Hall; Adams-Westfeldt Mine; Fontana Mine.

Chapter 5— Page 59
**THE RACE BEGINS**
Early Loggers; Splash Dams; Early Conservation Efforts; Roosevelt Report.

Chapter 6— Page 71
**MOUNTAIN RAILS**
Western North Carolina Railroad; Murphy Branch; Carolina and Tennessee Southern Railroad.

*Chapter 7— Page 79*
**THE BACK OF BEYOND BOOMS**
*Big Timber Companies; Logging Railroads; Kitchens & the Vivian; Ritter & Proctor.*

*Chapter 8— Page 109*
**BETTER LATE THAN NEVER**
*Early Preservation Attempts; Weeks Act Passed; Eastern Park Competition; Smokies Win; Fontana Area Excluded.*

*Chapter 9— Page 119*
**RIVER BECOMES RESOURCE**
*Aluminum needs the River; Alcoa builds first Dams.*

*Chapter 10— Page 131*
**DREAMERS WITH SHOVELS**
*TVA Established; Alcoa vs. TVA; War brings Agreement; TVA moves in and builds small town.*

*Chapter 11— Page 155*
**WORK OR FIGHT**
*Life at a War Project; Dam Kids; Attitude Equals Concrete; Big Brother Speaks; An Orchestra of Men and Machines.*

*Chapter 12— Page 181*
**THE CHANGE BACK**
*Land Acquisition; Reservoir Clearing; Road, Railroad, and Cemetery relocation; North Shore Road Controversy.*

*Chapter 13— Page 199*
**THE VILLAGE OF MANY LIVES**
*Here come the Millions; Horace Kephart; Tourists find Fontana.*

*Chapter 14— Page 221*
**APPALACHIAN CROSSROAD**
*Thoughts on the Future.*

*Page 227*
**SOURCES OF INFORMATION**
*Books; Papers; Interviews and Contributions; Maps; Periodicals; Catalogs; Videos.*

*Page 234*
**INDEX**

## INTRODUCTIONS

I've had the opportunity to work with Lance Holland on several projects, most notably a video entitled *Nantahala: Land of the Noonday Sun*. That documentary details the human and natural history of the Nantahala River, a well-known tributary of the Little Tennessee River. I was struck then by Lance's sincere interest in the mountain region he has chosen to make home, and I was impressed with his firm grasp of the regions cultural and economic history, dating from the arrival of the earliest Indians up to the present time. Across the board, he knew more about the nitty-gritty of the logging, mining, and hydroelectric industries than anyone I had previously encountered.

Moreover, he understood how those activities interfaced with the tourism boom that skyrocketed with the founding of the Great Smoky Mountains National Park. So, I wasn't surprised when Lance handed me the manuscript of *Fontana: A Pocket History of Appalachia* to discover that he has taken some of the video's themes and enlarged them to cover the history of the entire Little Tennessee region. Even those readers who already know a lot about these matters will be gratified to discover how much new ground has been broken herein—especially in the latter portions of the book where Lance enumerates matters in which he played a direct role.

Humor is always a precious commodity, particularly in historical narratives. There's humor aplenty in *Fontana*. All in all, it's a dandy book that will help folks who reside in or visit the area have a clearer understanding of just where they are.

George Ellison
Bryson City, North Carolina

This is a book that needed to be written, and I'm glad Lance has done it for he knows the Fontana area well, having lived and worked there for years. Several books have been written about the formation of the Great Smokies Park, and about the Fontana basin area in general, but none specifically about this "pocket" of southern Appalachia. Lance has done that, with archival material, folk memories, and information not found in any other book.

It is a long and complex history, from the first Indians to arrive several thousand years ago, through the 18th century traders, scientists looking for new plants, settlers looking for land, the forced removal of the Cherokees, loggers and miners reaping a rich harvest of trees and copper, the formation of the park, and finally, the building of a great dam whose lake flooded the Little Tennessee River valley and forced everyone to leave this pocket of land.

Throughout the book, Lance weaves the story of the Little Tennessee River, sacred to the Cherokees, useful to the early timbermen as a way to get their logs out, and finally, when dammed, to produce electricity for the manufacture of aluminum during World War II.

It's a storied land, and Lance tells its story well.

Duane Oliver
Hazelwood, North Carolina

## Chapter 1
# The Original People

As the first hints of grey light outlined the mountains above, Attakullakulla stood on the edge of the bluff known as the Narrows. Below he could hear the great river highway of the Cherokee people. White men would come to call the river the Little Tennessee, and the area around the Narrows would see many changes. Soldiers would come to build a fort to protect their Cherokee allies and then punish them for transgressions and then to try to capture the last few remaining Indians and send them on their way west on the infamous "Trail of Tears." White settlers would hack out a living in the forest primeval. A father of the Great Smoky Mountains National Park would come to find the "Back of Beyond." Lumber barons would transform the area from pioneer settlements to the forefront of American technology practically overnight. Large scale miners would bore into its very heart to extract valuable minerals. An army of workers would build a small city and a mammoth dam to help win World War II. Finally sportsmen and tourists would discover what Attakullakulla already knew—the area that would become Fontana is a very special place. But from time beyond memory the river had provided the Cherokees and the people preceeding them many things that were important to their way of life.

The settlements of the Cherokees (at about the time European traders and explorers first penetrated the interior of southeastern North America) have been grouped in three districts. The largest and first group to be affected by Europeans were called the Lower Cherokees. Their settlements encompassed much of the northern half of Georgia and northwest South Carolina. The second group were called the Middle Cherokees, with a primary town, Nikwasi, located near present day Franklin, North Carolina. One of the best preserved Indian mounds in the region is located alongside the

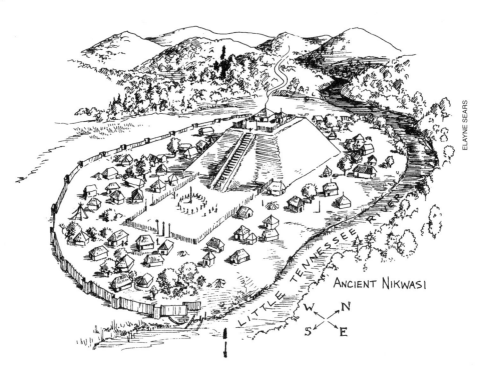

ANCIENT NIKWASI

Little T. at the site of Nikwasi. It is generally accepted that the Cherokees did not build earthen mounds but habitated and utilized these landscape improvements that were constructed basketful by basketful by Indian people who preceded them. Many other Indian towns prospered along the Little T. and its tributaries as it flowed westward toward the rampart of the Great Smoky and Unaka mountains. The third group were called the Overhill Cherokees. Their primary town was Chota, which was located near the confluence of the Little T. and Tellico rivers in east

Tennessee. Canoe travel and foot trails along the Little T. were a vital transportation link for the far-flung settlements of the Cherokee nation. From the Narrows westward to Chilhowee, the river sliced through the spine of the Great Smoky and Unaka Mountains. The resulting gorge was probably a dangerous and inhospitable area. Therefore, the overland trail that passed through Cheoah (present day Robbinsville, North Carolina) was an alternate route between the middle and overhill settlements.

The portion of western North Carolina occupied by the Middle Cherokees was a beautiful place. A trip today to Joyce Kilmer Memorial Forest (the largest virgin cove hardwood forest in the eastern U.S.) located northwest of Robbinsville will give the visitor a taste of what the forests of the region must have looked like in the late 18th century. William Bartram, botanist and explorer, described a visit to the town of Cowee in 1775 as follows:

> *Proceeding on our return to town, continued through part of this high forest skirting on the meadows: began to ascend the hills of a ridge which we were under the necessity of crossing; and having gained its summit, enjoyed a most enchanting view; a vast expanse of green meadows and strawberry fields; a meandering river gliding through, saluting in its various turnings the swelling, green, turfy knolls, embellished with parterres of flowers and fruitful strawberry beds; flocks of turkeys strolling about them; herds of deer prancing in the meads or bounding over the hills; companies of young, innocent Cherokee virgins, some busy gathering the rich fragrant fruit, others having already filled their baskets, lay reclined under the shade of floriferous and fragrant native bowers of Magnolia, Azalea, Philadelphus, perfumed Calycanthus, sweet Yellow Jessamine and cerulean Glycine frutescens, disclosing their beauties to the fluttering breeze, and bathing their limbs in the cool fleeting streams; whilst other parties, more gay and libertine, were yet collecting strawberries, or wantonly chasing their companions, tantalizing them, staining their lips and cheeks with the rich fruit.*

The Cherokees were "strongly attached to rivers, all retaining the opinion of the ancients that rivers are necessary to constitute a paradise," wrote British trader James Adair, who came to America in 1735 and spent 28 years among the southeastern Indians. Not only did the river provide food and transportation, it was part of

Cherokee religion and mythology and provided cures for illness. Fish, mussels, turtles, and eels were speared, caught on hooks, poisoned, and trapped to provide food. Fish traps were constructed by building two low stone walls from opposite sides of the river. The walls angled downstream, creating a funnel where cane baskets were placed. People then entered the river upstream of the trap and noisily waded downstream, driving the fish into the baskets. Remains of fish traps can be seen today in the Oconaluftee, Little T., and Tuckasegee Rivers.

**Cherokee girl grinding corn.**

The Cherokees were adept at fashioning dugout canoes from large trees. Tulip poplar (Lirondendron tulipefera) was the material of choice due to its straight trunk, buoyancy, and ease of working. The tree trunks were burned on one side so that the burnt material could be removed with stone axes; the process was repeated until a very river-worthy craft was created. Some canoes were up to 40 feet long and could transport 20 people. A demonstration of this ancient craft can be seen at the Oconaluftee Living Indian Village in Cherokee, North Carolina.

James Mooney spent three years among the Cherokees at the end of the 19th century to learn and record their myths. The result of this work was a 550 page "report" entitled *Myths of the Cherokee*. About half of the myths involve rivers. The Cherokee practice of "going to water" or submersion in the river was a religious ritual practiced to purify events such as birth, hunting, and war. If the dip in the cold river was preceded by a trip to the "asi," a small earth covered steam bath heated by hot rocks, "going to water" became the treatment for numerous ailments.

When European traders and longhunters first entered Cherokee country, the Cherokee nation claimed lands from near present day Orangeburg, South Carolina to Cincinnati, Ohio and from Wytheville, Virginia to Tuscumbia, Alabama. By the end of the American Revolution, the fertile South Carolina lands and the hunting grounds of Kentucky had been ceded to the relentless throng of land hungry Americans. The next 50 years saw a steady stream of "last" treaties ceding more and more land. By about 1830 Cherokee lands were confined to extreme southwestern North Carolina, southeastern Tennessee, northwestern Georgia, and northeastern Alabama. Between 1794 and 1819 alone, the U.S. Government pressed the Cherokees into making 24 treaties involving small and large land cessions.

The Cherokees became the most "civilized" of all Indian tribes. They adopted a constitution and viewed themselves as an autonomous nation. By the mid-1820's, many Cherokees could read and write using the Cherokee alphabet that had been invented by Sequoyah. In 1828, the first issue of the *Cherokee Phoenix* newspaper was published.

Since 1802, the state of Georgia had been pressing the U.S. Government to expel the Cherokee from that state. The discovery of gold near Auroria, Georgia in 1828 brought the situation to a head. Much legal maneuvering was done by both Georgia and the Cherokees. Finally the Supreme Court

***Sequoyah.***

said that Georgia had no jurisdiction over the remaining lands of the Cherokee. President Andrew Jackson's reaction to this was "Justice Marshal has made his decision, now let him enforce it." Years before Jackson made this statement, Chief Junaluska, who resided at the site of present day Robbinsville, and his Cherokee warriors had turned the tide at the Battle of Horseshoe Bend in favor of General Andrew Jackson's forces. After repeated unsuccessful frontal attacks by Jackson's troops on the fortifications defended by the Creek Indians on a peninsula in a deep bend in the Tallapoosa River, Junaluska swam the river, stole the Creek's canoes and ferried his Cherokee warriors across to stage a successful rear attack and routed the Creeks. It is said that Junaluska personally saved Jackson's life during the battle. Junaluska migrated to Oklahoma during the removal but later walked back to his home in North Carolina. In 1847, the North Carolina legislature granted citizenship to Junaluska and deeded him 337 acres of land that would later become Robbinsville, North Carolina. He was also given $100 for his service to his country. After the removal, Junaluska was often heard to say, "If I had known that Jackson would drive us from our homes, I would have killed him that day at the Horseshoe." Junaluska's grave in Robbinsville is marked by a large boulder and plaque placed in 1910 by the Joseph Winston Chapter of the Daughters of the American Revolution.

On December 29, 1835, The Treaty of New Echota was signed by Major Ridge, his college educated son John, *Cherokee Phoenix* editor Elias Boudinot, and other Cherokee leaders who were primarily motivated by economic and political ambition. The treaty was not supported by the vast majority of the Cherokees. In fact, almost 15,000 members of the tribe signed a petition protesting that the treaty was initiated by an unauthorized minority. The U.S. Senate ratified it anyway and it went into effect. This treaty stipulated that all Cherokee people "shall remove to their new homes within two years from the ratification of the treaty." These new homes were in the Indian Territory which is now the state of Oklahoma.

By early 1838 several thousand Cherokees had traveled west on their own. The processions organized by the government via riverboats and overland trails were not producing the desired results, so in April 1838, it was decided that soldiers would be needed to effect the removal. General Winfield Scott was placed in command. By May, Scott had established headquarters at New Echota, Georgia and had assembled an army of seven thousand men in the four states. Large departure points were established at Ross' Landing near Chattanooga, Tennessee and Gunters' Landing at Gunterville, Alabama, both on the Tennessee River. Smaller forts or stockades were erected throughout the Cherokee country. Fort Montgomery at present day Robbinsville and Fort Lindsay at the present day Almond Boat Dock served the area that would become Fontana.

Although several trails existed from the Little T. southward, they were too rough and steep to accommodate heavy wagons. Therefore a military road was surveyed and constructed by soldiers under the command of Captain W.G. Wiliams to provide access from Fort Delaney near present day Andrews, North Carolina to the sites of Fort Montgomery and Fort Lindsey. The road left Fort Delaney and headed west crossing the mountains near Joanna Bald at Tatham Gap and descended via Long Creek and passed through Cheoah (present day Robbinsville) at Fort Montgomery. This section of the road is known today as Tatham Gap Road and much of it is little changed from the days of removal. The road then followed Sweetwater Creek up and over Stecoah Gap, across Stecoah valley, through Gunter Gap, down Wolf Creek and Panther Creek, and crossed a low ridge to join the Little Tennessee Turnpike near the place where the town of Judson would be situated years later.

There is evidence that as early as 1780, herds of livestock from the Tennessee Valley were driven up the old river road/trail to the market in Charleston, South Carolina. Joe (Joseph) Welch took out land near present day Franklin around 1820 where he had a store/trading post. A real entrepreneur, Welch got the contract to build a road down the Little T. from Franklin towards Big Bear's place on the Tuckaseegee river (which later became Charleston and then Bryson City). Soon after the Cherokees ceded the area north of the Little T., he took out land in 1828 at the confluence of the Little T. and the Tukaseegee rivers, a place that later became the town of Bushnell. Seeing a chance to make more money and having experience as a road-builder, in 1832 he borrowed $1200 and sold some slaves to build a turnpike/toll road from Bushnell down the river to the state line at Deals Gap. Welch never made much money from this venture for he declared bankruptcy in 1848.

Systems were in place and the actual removal of the Cherokees began in June 1838. Apparently the removal in North Carolina went smoothly because on July 21, 1838, General Scott withdrew the soldiers in the area after being assured by General Eustis that all North Carolina Cherokees subject to removal had been removed. The Treaty of 1819 had granted citizenship and lands to about 500 Cherokees living along the Oconaluftee River. This area was ceded in 1819 and was not part of Cherokee lands in

1838. The 500 Oconaluftee Indians or "Citizen" Cherokees—under the guidance of a white trader, William Holland Thomas, who had come to the nation as a small boy and was subsequently adopted by the great Chief Yonaguska—were not subject to removal.

**William Holland Thomas, white chief of the Cherokees.**

In early August, General Scott learned that about 300 Indians were hiding in the mountains in the vicinity of what would become the Fontana area. Scott sent four detachments of mounted troops to scour the region and capture as many fugitives as possible. By the end of October, three of the detachments had left the area and Second Lieutenant A.J. Smith and his men, escorted by Will Thomas, were headed west along the Little Tennessee Turnpike toward Tennessee with 15 captured Cherokee. It seemed that the horrible episode of Cherokee removal from their homeland was over. Enter Tsali.

If there was a competition for stories that "get better with the tellin," the story of Tsali would be in the Olympics. Tsali or "Old Charley" has been characterized as everything from a martyr to a murderer by whites and Indians alike. Most of the early published accounts of the Tsali episode were based on interviews of Will Thomas. In Thomas' latter years he suffered both financial and mental breakdown and actually spent time in mental hospitals. One of the first written accounts was published in 1849 by Charles Lanman. In his *Letters From The Allegheny Mountains*, Lanman praised Tsali for his sacrifice for the good of his people. Forty years later James Mooney also interviewed Will Thomas. His account in *Myths of the Cherokee* varied substantially from Lanman's. Mooney's version of the story is probably the basis for many modern recounts. He described the events as follows:

All were not submissive. One old man named Tsali, "Charley" was seized with his wife, his brother, his three sons and their families. Exasperated at the brutality accorded his wife, who, being unable to travel fast, was prodded with bayonets to hasten her steps, he urged the other men to join with him in a dash for liberty. As he spoke in Cherokee the soldiers, although they heard, understanding nothing until each warrior suddenly sprang upon the nearest and endeavored to wrench his gun from him. The attack was so sudden and unexpected that one soldier was killed and the rest fled, while the Indians escaped to the mountains. Hundreds of others, some of them from the various stockades, managed also to escape to the mountains from time to time, where those who did not die of starvation subsisted on roots and wild berries until the hunt was over. Finding it impracticable to secure these fugitives, General Scott finally tendered them a proposition through (Colonel) W.H. Thomas, their most trusted friend, that if they would surrender Charley and his party for punishment, the rest would be allowed to remain until their case could be adjusted by the government. On hearing of the proposition, Charley voluntarily came in with his sons, offering himself as a sacrifice for his people. By command of General Scott, Charley, his brother, and the two elder sons were shot near the mouth of Tuckasegee, a detachment of Cherokee prisoners being compelled to do the shooting in order to impress upon the Indians the fact of their utter helplessness. From those fugitives thus permitted to remain, originated the present eastern band of Cherokee.

In 1979, Duane King and E. Raymond Evans researched the actual military records concerning the final days of Cherokee removal and reported their findings about Tsali in volume IV, number 4 of the *Journal of Cherokee Studies* published by the Museum of the Cherokee Indian. Their synopsis of this research reads:

*A number of primary documents, some of which are previously unpublished, are presented in this issue to help elucidate an important part of Cherokee heritage. As will be noted, the Tsali incident is not as much of a mystery as some writers have maintained. From the documents presented in this volume and others, the following sequence of events can be reconstructed with a reasonable degree of certainty.*

**Dec. 29, 1835**—*Treaty of New Echota, ceding all remaining Cherokee Territory east of the Mississippi, signed.*

**May 23, 1836**—Treaty of New Echota was ratified by the Senate, with the Cherokees being given two years in which to peaceably remove.

**Feb. 8, 1838**—Capt. W. G. Williams, U.S. Army Topographic Engineer Corps, reports that the Cherokees in western North Carolina remain steadfastly adverse to removal, and that the terrain and the possible collusion with the "Citizen Cherokees" could afford the strong possibility for resistance.

**May 10**—Gen. Scott established military headquarters at New Echota and called upon the Cherokees to come in for removal.

**June 8**—Forced removal began.

**July 21**—General Scott ordered the 1st Infantry Regiment from North Carolina to the Canadian Frontier after being assured by General Eustis that all Cherokees within the Cherokee Nation in limits of North Carolina had been removed.

**Early Aug**—Scott learned that around 300 fugitives were hidden in the mountains and ordered Lieutenant Scott, with mounted troops and Indian runners into the mountains.

**Sept. 12**—Lieutenants Larned, Johnson and Smith were ordered to the mountains with reinforcements.

**Oct. 29**—Second Lieutenant A.J. Smith, with a detachment of the 1st Dragoons, accompanied by W.H. Thomas, escorted 15 Cherokees captured at Pickens Courthouse down the Tuckasegee River.

**Oct. 30**—Upon learning of the presence of additional fugitives near the mouth of the Tuckasegee, Smith divided his command, and captured 12 members of Tsali's family.

**Oct. 31**—Smith learned that the 15 captives from Pickens Courthouse had escaped from his sergeant and hurried Tsali's family ahead to overtake the rest of his command. W.H. Thomas remained behind due to an unexplained accident.

**Nov. 1**—Tsali's family escaped from Smith, killing 2 soldiers (Parry and (evening)Martin), and seriously injuring another (Gutty). Smith escaped on horseback.

**Nov. 5**—Smith reported the incident to Lieutenant Larned. Larned immediately reported the matter to General Scott.

**Nov. 7**—General Scott ordered Colonel William S. Foster with the 4th Infantry to search for the fugitives and punish the murderers.

**Nov. 11**—Captain McCall with "C" Company, accompanied by two Indian guides, left to examine the length of Deep Creek.

**Nov. 12**—Fourth Infantry set up camp at Joe Welch's on the Little Tennessee. Lieutenant Larned left with a mounted company accompanied by W.H. Thomas to look for Tsali along the Oconeelufty. He was instructed to join a patrol of Captain McCall.

**Nov. 12**—Captain Morris with "H" Company went out to examine the Little Tennessee and Nantahala Rivers.

**Nov. 15**—Lieutenants Prince and Graham with "D" and "K" Companies were sent out with two additional detachments led by sergeants to check the countryside.

**Nov. 18**—Colonel Foster received a petition from area whites requesting that Euchella's band be permitted to remain in North Carolina.

**Nov. 19**—Colonel Foster reported to General Scott the capture of the murderers, Nantayalee Jake, Tsali's oldest son and Nantayalee George, the husband of Tsali's daughter Ancih. He also reported the capture of Tsali's wife (old Nancy) and George's wife and daughter. He further reported that Euchella's band, the Oconulufty Indians, and a mounted company were in close pursuit of the remaining murderers.

**Nov. 21**—A board of inquiry was convened to identify the accused murderers, Jake, George, and Lowan; the latter had been captured since the 19th. The witnesses against them were Lieutenant Smith, W.H. Thomas, and Joe Welch.

**Nov. 23**—George, Jake, and Lowan were executed by the Nantahala under Euchella. A younger male, whom Thomas later identified as Wasseton, was spared because of his youth.

**Nov. 24**—Colonel Foster reports to General Scott that his mission has been accomplished. He issued a proclamation exempting Euchella and his band from removal in consideration for his assistance in the search for the murderers. Colonel Foster and the 4th Infantry then departed from North Carolina.

**Nov. 25**—Tsali is captured and executed by Euchella and Wachacha near Big Bear's reserve on the Tuckasegee.

***Dec. 3***—*Colonel Foster defended his action in permitting Euchella and his band to remain with the Oconulufty Indians in a letter to General Scott.*

***Dec. 28***—*General Scott commends the action of Colonel Foster and the 4th Infantry to Brigadier General R. Jones, Adj. General of the Army.*

***Jan. 4, 1839***—*Colonel Foster is cited by the War Department for his "gallantry, and perseverance displayed in the pursuit and capture of the Indians who had cruelly murdered two soldiers of the Regiment."*

Regardless of exactly how the events concerning the capture and execution unfolded, the results were the same. Colonel William S. Foster issued a proclamation on November 24, 1838 from Camp Scott located at the farm of Joe Welch on the Little T. that stated "in consideration of his recent good actions in pursuing, capturing, delivering, and finally punishing, the outlaws and murderers of Charley's band grant to him the aforesaid chief, Euchella,

**Trail of tears.**

ROBERT LINDNEUX 1840

his Brother (Wachacha), and all others of his band as aforesaid, my permission to live in this country as associates and brothers of the Oconelufty Indians ." The census of 1840 showed that about 1,000 Cherokees (500 "citizen" and 500 "fugitive") had avoided removal and became the core of the Eastern Band of Cherokee Indians.

It is pertinent to note at this point in our journey that the Cherokees were just the first people to be forcibly removed by the U.S. Government from the Fontana area. Next, railroad companies armed with the "writ of eminent domain" would force people to sell their land for the common progress. Then finally, the Tennessee Valley Authority in conjunction with the National Park Service armed with the ultimate "writ of eminent domain" would almost completely depopulate the entire Fontana area.

*Chapter 2*
# The First Europeans

The Fontana area was settled by white people very late in the time line of American history, but the area hosted early explorers soon after they arrived on the continent. Hernando De Soto and his men crossed the Little Tennessee River in 1540. Historians disagree on his exact route, but it is not probable that the expedition ventured down the Little T. as far as Fontana. In 1567 another group of gold-seeking Spaniards led by Juan Pardo did enter the region. There is strong evidence that Pardo camped at the middle town of Kituwha located on the banks of the Tuckasegee River about two miles upstream from present day Bryson City, North Carolina.

The next to come were the English, who were seeking fortunes in furs rather than gold. On July 15, 1673, two white men, James Needham and Gabriel Arthur, arrived at the overhill town of Chota. They had been sent by Abraham Wood, a Virginia trader, to establish a trade link between the Cherokees and the Virginia Colony. Although the trade link did not materialize due to interference from other Indian tribes, Gabriel Arthur did live with the Cherokees at Chota for about a year. Arthur accompanied Cherokee war parties on raids throughout the southeast. Therefore it is most probable that he was the first Englishman to pass through the Fontana area.

Undoubtedly, other explorer/traders followed close behind. The Cherokees, who had previously only hunted for food and skins

W.H. POWELL 1868

**DeSoto discovers the Mississippi.**

for clothing and believed strongly in the natural balance of things, were quickly caught up in the commerce of the day. By 1700, a regular flow of trade goods from the Cherokees such as animal hides, particularly deerskins, beeswax, and bear oil were arriving in Charleston, South Carolina for export to England. English export records show that in 1708 about 50,000 deerskins were shipped annually from Charleston, and by 1735 over one million white tail deer had given their all for Mother England.

    One of the more colorful white men to venture into the Cherokee country very early on was Sir Alexander Cuming, a Scotsman who has been characterized as a promoter, showman, con-man, genius, and fool. In March of 1730, Cuming and a small entourage left Charleston bound for Cherokee country. Cuming had a plan. After preliminary meetings with regional chiefs all over the Cherokee nation, he arranged a big rendezvous at Nikwasi (present day

Franklin) on April 3, 1730. Chiefs and headmen from across the nation gathered at the council house atop the Nikwasi mound. The leaders at hand were quite taken with Cuming—it was reputed that at Cuming's request they knelt and acknowledged King George II as their ruler. The next part of the plan was for Cuming to establish himself as the key to an alliance between the Cherokees and the British. To accomplish this, he persuaded seven chiefs, including Attakullakulla—who occasionally lived in the Fontana area—to accompany him to London and visit with none other than King George himself. The experienced traders that had come with Cuming to Indian country were totally amazed at the Scotsman's audacity and even more amazed by his success.

Cuming and his colorful group of Indians arrived in London in June 1730 and immediately became the toast of the town. The English had long thought that an alliance with the Cherokee people was imperative to protect their colonies on the Atlantic seaboard from an overland attack by the French and their Indian allies. The group dined with the King and presented him gifts from their homeland. In return, the King directed England's Board of Trade and Plantations in America to give the Cherokees "gifts" to take home. These included guns, gunpowder, bullets, flints, hatchets, folding knives, and brass kettles. Acceptance of the gifts required that the Cherokees "shall not suffer their people to trade with the white men of any other nation but the English." The seven Indians returned to the Little T. burdened with their gifts and trade flourished. The Cherokees were not as exclusive in regard to their trading partners as the British had hoped—but, nevertheless, a bond had been established between the Crown and the mighty Cherokee nation.

In 1754, at the request of the Cherokees, English authorities agreed to build a fort in the far western reaches of their country to help protect the inhabitants from the French and their Indian allies. Fort Loudon would be the westernmost outpost of the British colonies. Due to bureaucratic bungling, the main body of fort builders did not reach the site until September 1756. For the 250 soldiers dispatched to construct the fort, the Fontana area was a vast wild land that had to be traversed to reach their objective. A trader named John Elliott had an even more arduous task. He was contracted to transport 12 cannons across the mountains to arm the fort. When Elliott reached the fort with all 12 cannons intact (although one blew up in an artilleryman's face at its first firing), he was asked how he accomplished this feat. "Mainstrength and awkwardness," he replied.

Soon after the fort was completed, relations between the Cherokees and the English started to deteriorate. A series of unfortunate incidents in which both Indians and whites died caused tensions to escalate. An attempt to resurrect the peace by Chief Oconostota was rejected by the British. The British sent a force of 1500 men under Colonel Archibald Montgomery to punish the Cherokees and rescue the soldiers besieged at Fort Loudon. Oconostota's warriors ambushed them near Nikwasi and routed Montgomery's forces. The British turned back to Charleston.

Finally on August 9, 1760, the soldiers at Fort Loudon surrendered the fort to the Cherokees and were allowed to return to

**Sir Alexander Cuming's entourage for England in 1730, Attakullaculla is at the far right.**

Charleston. As the 180 men and 60 women broke camp their first morning on the trail to Charleston, the Indians massacred many of them, especially the officers. Historians cannot explain this action, although the episode was quite similar to the surrender of Fort Prince George during the French and Indian War as depicted in James Fenemore Cooper's novel and the 1993 movie *"The Last of the Mohicans."* Employing a sort of eye for an eye, tooth for a tooth rationale, the Cherokees once again sued for peace. British General Jeffery Amherst was not receptive to say the least. He dispatched Colonel James Grant and 2000 veteran infantrymen fresh from their victory in the French and Indian war to punish the Cherokees once and for all. Chief Oconostota repeated his ambush attempt but despite heavy losses, Colonel Grant prevailed. He proceeded to lay waste to Indian towns along the Little T., Tuckasegee, Nantahala, and Cheoah Rivers. This was probably the first time the Cherokees retreated to the mountain fastness of the Fontana and Smoky Mountain region to escape the onslaught of white soldiers.

On September 23, 1761, Attakullakulla, who had become the peace chief of the Cherokees, signed a treaty with Governor Bull and ended the hostilities. These events and those described heretofore resulted in the inevitable demise of the great Cherokee nation.

The first official tourist to visit the area was my good friend, Little Billy Bartram, who came to botanize and explore in the spring of 1776. Okay, William Bartram the noted botanist who discovered and named hundreds of plants in the southeast and recorded his explorations in a delightful book entitled *Travels of William Bartram* was not really a friend, but I do feel a kinship. Over the years I have had the privilege to guide numerous groups from the prestigious Bartram Society to find the places and plants that were so eloquently described in *Travels*. The Bartram Society maintains extensive gardens in Philadelphia, showcasing many of the botanical discoveries of William Bartram. One memorable trip involved unloading a group of well-to-do pilgrims from their luxury motorcoach and loading them into the back of my pick-up truck. It was 45 degrees and raining lightly. The chagrined tour operator stood silently as I carted off her well-paying charges into the wilderness. The trails in Joyce Kilmer Memorial Forest with their giant trees, profusions of wildflowers, and riotous streams completely enthralled the pilgrims. Upon our return to the motorcoach, the elated but soggy group thanked me profusely for showing and letting them experience the mountains that Billy had so enjoyed rather than the garden where William preserved plants.

William Bartram was sponsored by his botanist father, John Bartram, who had established the first botanical garden in America at Philadelphia. John's friend Benjamin Franklin and the Royal Society of London also provided support for William's expedition through southeastern America to "present new as well as useful information to the botanist and zoologist." In May 1776, William arrived at the middle town of Cowee, located about four miles up the Little T. from Nikwasi. Bartram was quite taken by Cowee and wrote glowingly about his stay there. From Cowee, his route to the Overhill towns would lead him through the big wild mountains, much different from the pleasant river valleys he had followed from Charleston. The traders he had conferred with before leaving the lowlands had warned him not to proceed past Cowee without a guide and protector and had arranged for such a person to meet Bartram at Cowee. But after waiting two days for the guide to arrive, William "resolved to pursue the journey alone." Rather than follow the trading path as he left Cowee, Bartram was "determined at all events to cross the Jore Mountain, said to be the highest land in the Cherokee country." Today the Jore Mountains are called the Nantahalas and "the most elevated peak from whence I beheld with rapture and astonishment a sublimely awful scene of power and magnificence, a world of mountains piled upon mountains" was somewhere in the vicinity of Wayah Bald.

Continuing west, Bartram followed the headwaters of the Nantahala River and about where the present day rafting put-in near the Nantahala power house is located, he met well-mounted Indians traveling rapidly toward him. The group was led by Attakullakulla, who was on one of his peace missions to Charleston. After exchanging greetings, Attakullakulla and his men rode off toward Charleston and Bartram continued toward the Overhill towns. That afternoon—"upon serious consideration, it appearing very plainly that I could not, with entire safety, range the overhill settlements"—Bartram decided to "return to Dartmouth in Georgia, to be ready to join a company of adventurers who were to set off in July for Mobile in west Florida."

The next day Bartram returned to Cowee and that evening attended a big pep rally held at the council house for the stickball game to be held the following day. Stickball is sort of a cross between field hockey, lacrosse, and tackle football with no pads. The game is so rough that the referees have switches with which to beat offending players. Ball-plays were held between towns, clans, and even tribes, with the winners receiving everything from bragging rights to thousands of acres of hunting lands. Modern Cherokees have preserved the game and if you ever have the opportunity to see one, you will not regret it.

Of course neither Bartram nor the Indians participating called the gathering a "pep rally," but as Bartram described the events of the evening the similarities are striking: "This assembly was held principally to rehearse the ball-play dance, this town being challenged to play against another the next day." First the coach gives a pep talk: "The people being assembled and seated in order, and the musicians having taken their station, the ball opens, first with a long harangue or oration, spoken by an aged chief, in commendation of the manly exercise of the ball-play, recounting the many and brilliant victories which the town of Cowee had gained over the other towns in the nation, not forgetting or neglecting to re-

**Stickball game in 1932.**

cite his own exploits, together with those of other aged men now present, coadjutors in the performance of these athletic games in their youthful days." Next a rousing song or two from the band: "This prologue being at an end, the musicians began, both vocal and instrumental." Enter the cheerleaders: "When presently a company of girls, hand in hand, dressed in clean white robes and ornamented with beads, bracelets and a profusion of gay ribbands, entering the door, immediately began to sing their responses." And finally the triumphant entrance of the players themselves: "We were surprised by a sudden very loud and shrill whoop, uttered at once by a company of young fellows, who came in briskly after one another, with rackets or hurls in one hand. These champions likewise were well dressed, painted, and ornamented with silver bracelets, gorgets and wampum, neatly ornamented with moccasins and high waving plumes in their diadems." I feel sure, in my heart, that Cowee won the game.

Other botanists such as John Fraser, Andre Michaux, and Asa Grey would come to explore the southern highlands. More traders and government officials would penetrate the mountain fastness to attend to their business. And finally, after most of the more level and accessible lands of the southeast and fertile bottom land of the foothills had been taken out by their forefathers, a few hardy white settlers started to trickle into the Fontana area.

**Cherokee ball player.**

## The First Europeans 31

UNTO THESE HILLS

18th Century Cherokee Village (above). Walini, a Cherokee woman (right). A Cherokee plows with yoke of oxen (below).

## Chapter 3
# Settlers Trickle In

As the tide of American settlement expanded westward during the 18th and 19th centuries, the southern side of the Smoky Mountains seemed to be an undiscovered island. Prior to the Treaty of 1819 only a few traders lived in the Fontana area. By that treaty, the Cherokees ceded all lands north of the Little Tennessee River and east of the Nantahala Mountains. These lands were divided into 640 acre tracts and offered for sale by the government for between five and ten cents per acre. Much of the land was purchased by speculators who did not occupy the land but hoped to sell to settlers for a profit or exploit the land for its natural resources. A few very early settlers, however, had bought land from the Indians.

Captain W.G. Williams described the region in February 1838 as follows:

> The mountains are generally clothed with woods to their summits, with but a few exceptions, called bald mountains, but the vallies having been subjected to cultivation, by the Indians from time immemorial, are almost entirely devoid of timber, and where not actually tilled are partially overgrown with oak, coppice. The forests are generally very open, that is, the trees are wide apart, and the fires which the Indians continually make to burn the undergrowth or brush, in order to facilitate hunting, remove the obstructions which it could otherwise present to a free passage in all directions...a few white families only have been able to gain a footing in this country.

The first tracts to be occupied by white settlers were the large level river valleys. One of the earliest settlements was along the Oconaluftee River and its tributaries. Records show an election was held on Soco Creek, a tributary of the Oconaluftee, in 1809. Polly Sherrill Conley and her husband opened a little trading post at the mouth of Soco Creek around 1814. Most of her customers were Cherokees and a small settlement grew up around the store. There are no "B" or "P" sounds in the Cherokee language, so, unable to pronounce Polly, they called her "Qually." The little settlement became known as Qually's Town or Quallatown. Some other early settlers on the Oconaluftee were John Mingus, Robert Collins, Isaac Bradley, and Abraham Enloe. The Pioneer Farmstead Museum at the Oconaluftee Visitors Center is the site of Abraham Enloe's farm. Local legend persists that Abraham Enloe, a very prosperous man, was the father of Abraham Lincoln. Nancy Hanks, Lincoln's mother, was indeed a servant at the Enloe home prior to Lincoln's birth.

**Nantahala, Valley of the Noonday Sun.**

The broad and fertile valley lands were rather quickly "taken-up," forcing newcomers and offspring of the early settlers to look "further up the hollow" for lands of their own. Many families actually had "weaner cabins" on the farm where young couples would live until they could build a cabin and clear land of their own. The stories of Moses and Patience Proctor and Jessie and Catherine Gunter provide good examples of what pioneer settlers throughout the Appalachians experienced.

Moses and Patience Proctor and their first child William were living in Cades Cove over the mountain in Tennessee near

Patience's family around 1829. The 50 or so families homesteading there made Cades Cove too crowded for Moses, so he set out to find uncrowded and cheaper land. His search took him across the top of the Smoky Mountains and down alongside the waters of Hazel Creek. The spot he chose for his cabin was about three miles north of where Hazel Creek emptied into the Little Tennessee River and was located in the center of where the Proctor Cemetery is today. The site was on top of a knoll that overlooked the creek and the main trail that went up the creek, but a considerable distance from the spring and the farm fields.

Much discussion has occurred among area historians as to why he picked this spot since pioneer settlers usually did not have "a good view" on their lists of criteria for picking a homesite. Given the fact that only a few Indian families and no white settlers lived along the creek, it could have been that the defensibility of this location could have worked in its favor. But given the fact that Mose's dying wish was to be buried in the "dooryard" of his first cabin, which became the first grave in the Proctor Cemetery, might lead one to conclude that the youthful Moses really did like the view; and besides, Patience would have to carry the water anyway. Since the cabin site was only about 20 miles from his first residence in Cades Cove, not a long walk in pioneer days, it is probable that some of Patience's family helped

***Joe Queen cabin, now at the Oconaluftee Pioneer Farmstead.***

build the cabin, and it was close to completion before the family actually moved over. A field cleared by Indians was just down the hill from the cabin that allowed planting of the first year's crop.

To expand or create cropland, pioneers used a technique called "deadening." This procedure involved chopping a ring through the bark and cambian layer of standing timber. The cambian layer just inside the bark contains the vessels that transport nutrients up and down the tree. Cutting through this layer severs the lifeline of the tree and causes it to die. In the spring, the lifeless standing timber allowed light to reach the fertile ground beneath where corn and other crops were planted. As time and labor allowed, some of these dead trees were used for buildings and fencing, but most were cut and piled at communal events called log rollings and then burned.

**After corn crops, girdled forests became pasture.**

U.S. DEPARTMENT OF AGRICULTURE

After shelter for the family was provided and the first crops were planted, attention turned to construction of a barn, fences, and other outbuildings. It would be five years before the next white family, Samuel and Elizabeth Cable, also coming from Cades Cove, would settle on Hazel Creek. Therefore, Moses and Patience and their small children had to fabricate almost everything they needed. Undoubtedly, the return trip from the occasional visit to Cades Cove or up the river to other settlements found the Proctors loaded with trade goods.

By the onset of the Civil War, only five or six families were living on Hazel Creek. All seven of the able-bodied men living on the creek, including four of Mose's sons, enlisted in the Confederate Army. The women, children, and old men left on the creek endured great hardship during the Civil War as did people all over the south. The Fontana area actually experienced a period of population growth during the war. Some families migrated to the mountains from areas more directly involved in the fighting. Deserters and renegades also found the mountain fastness a safe haven.

Toward the end of the war, Moses somehow found out that his oldest son William was badly wounded and stranded in Georgia. The 68 year old Moses set out to bring his boy home. After several weeks out in the elements, Moses and William returned to Hazel Creek. William's wounds healed with time, but Moses died not long after their return. Since there were no healthy men left on the creek, he was wrapped in a blanket and buried on the hill where his first cabin once stood. This was the first grave in what would become the largest graveyard in the Great Smoky Mountains National Park. All that was left on Hazel Creek for many years to mark the passing of Moses and Patience Proctor were two unmarked fieldstone headstones. In 1993, decendants of Moses and Patience placed a memorial at the grave site, but left the original fieldstones. Even the bustling lumber town of Proctor, named after the original settler, is nothing more than a memory.

When the Proctors moved to Hazel Creek in 1830, almost everyone in the Appalachians and a large percentage of all Americans were living on the "Frontier." In 1875, when Jessie Gunter decided to homestead in Welch Cove, America was a much different place. The Civil War had changed the complexion of America more than any event in history: passenger trains were running from New York to San Francisco; the industrial age was cranking up in American cities; the trading posts at Knoxville and Asheville had become bustling towns with rail service at the former and only a few miles from the latter; and Graham and Swain counties had been chartered in the mountains of far western North Carolina. But Welch Cove, where Fontana Village would later be built, was certainly still the frontier—only a rude sled trail provided access to the three families that lived there.

Although the Whiting Manufacturing Company had constructed and operated a logging railroad around the cove for a few years in the 1920's, it remained quite remote. When TVA surveyors arrived in 1940 to change the cove forever, only six families lived there—half the houses were log cabins and a rutted wagon road led to the outside world. Other families lived in Welch Cove for short periods. Many southern mountaineers accustomed to a pioneering lifestyle settled areas of the far west as those lands became available. Josiah Welch, for whom the cove was named, was one of these perennial pioneers. It has been said that all a mountain pioneer needed to do to prepare for a move across miles of wilderness was put out the fire and call the dogs.

Jessie Gunter was one of eight children born to Hiram and Bettie Gunter who lived in the prosperous farm community of Stecoah Valley. Jessie was a young man still living and working on the family farm when a new school marm arrived at the small Stecoah School. Nancy Catherine Richardson was born in South

**William Crow Proctor, son of Moses and Patience Proctor.**

GEORGE MASA

**Bone Valley schoolhouse.**

Carolina, raised and educated in Asheville, and must have been a bit adventurous to leave home and take a teaching job in the wilds of the Smokies. A classic book and popular television series, *Christy*, tells the story of another young Asheville teacher's experiences in the backcountry.

Soon Jessie and Catherine were courting and then married. By 1875 when Jessie walked over to Welch Cove to visit his brother Cyrene who lived there, the young couple had four children. Jessie probably followed the old Indian trails across the numerous side ridges of Yellow Creek Mountain on his first trip from Stecoah to Welch Cove. But when he moved the family over, they most likely followed the river, possibly by boat, to the mouth of Welch Cove Branch then up the trail to their new homeplace. The other access to the area from the river was an extremely steep trail called the Cat Stairs that had been hacked into the bluff near the Narrows.

Jessie and Cyrene Gunter were arguably two of the best carpenters in the Smokies. Ed Trout, retired chief historian for the Great Smoky Mountains National Park and author of *Historic Build-*

*ings of the Smokies,* said the one and one-half story log cabin that still stands today in the center of Fontana Village "is a finer example of dovetail craftmenship than any buildings left in the park." The cabin today houses a museum showcasing the rich history of Fontana and, with the exception of an anteroom and porch added to the eastside and a few replacement parts, is much like Jessie built it.

The brothers first felled large, straight tulip poplar trees and dragged them to the site. The logs were peeled and split using axe, maul, and wedges, then smoothed on two sides with a broadaxe and foot adze. They were then joined with near-perfect half dovetail notches to form the walls of the cabin. Other shorter slabs of poplar and cherry were hewn into puncheons, some two feet wide, that would be laid on squared joists to become the floor in the two downstairs rooms. Jessie would later remove and use some of these broad flat puncheons for a far different purpose. The loft or upstairs of the cabin was floored with boards that were

***Jessie Gunter Cabin.***

LANCE HOLLAND COLLECTION

created with the same splitting techniques and further smoothed with a drawknife to such a fine finish that only close inspection will reveal that they were not sawmill lumber. To connect the two floors, a magnificently simple staircase was fabricated. Massive stringers were hewn from green timber and mortises or slots were cut into them to accept the tennons, or projections on the ends of the step treads that had been crafted from well cured timber. The staircase was assembled using no nails, pegs, or glue—and as the green stringers dried, they shrunk around the tenons, creating joints that are still sound 120 years later. Roof boards or wooden shingles were rived or split from log sections of straight-grain white oak to cover the building. A good white oak roof would last twenty years. Needless to say, the Gunter cabin has been reroofed many times.

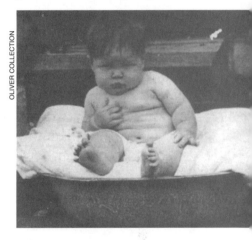

The next eight years saw the Gunter family prosper. Two more children were born to the couple and all the kids developed under the guidance of their craftsman father and well educated mother. Then one dreadful night in February 1884, as a blizzard raged outside, their world started to fall apart. Bettie, 10, and Hiram, 14, had been gravely ill for several days. A few other kids in the community were also sick. No one knew the name of this mysterious disease or how to best combat the high fever, rash, and congestion. The closest doctor was in Charleston, North Carolina (now named Bryson City) 40 miles away and the terrible weather prevented sending for him. Late on the night of February 24, 1884, as Catherine sat at her side, Bettie died. Bettie was simply left in her bed until the howling blizzard subsided to allow burial. Around midnight on February 27th, Hiram also succumbed to the terrible disease. The children were laid out in the back room and the fire extinguished as the rest of the family huddled around the fireplace in the other room through the long night.

The next morning, Catherine was awakened by the sounds of hammering coming from the room where the dead children lay.

When Catherine opened the door between the two rooms, she saw Jessie taking up some of the broad floor puncheons. He looked at her and said, "I'll not bury my boy and girl in no greenwood coffin and this is the only dry lumber I've got." Jessie constructed a strong coffin wide enough for both children. He and Catherine draped the inside with their best blankets and Bettie and Hiram were placed inside, side by side. The next day they were buried on top of the knoll across the valley from the cabin. Theirs was the first grave in the Welch Cove Cemetery located today at the end of Fontana Road in Fontana Village. Jessie made new puncheons to replace the coffin boards which are still in the cabin today.

**Fitting puncheons to floor joists.**

The death of the children affected Catherine very deeply. She tried to busy herself with the other kids and even taught school again from time to time. Nothing seemed to extinguish the terrible memories of those cold February nights in 1884. After several years, her depression worsened and on November 21, 1888, at the age of fifty-one, Catherine died in her sleep. This time Jessie removed the cherry wood puncheons from the front room and built a fine coffin for his beloved Catherine. She was buried in the graveyard alongside her children.

By this time the charm of Welch Cove had worn off for Jessie. He sold the cabin in its floorless condition and moved back to Stecoah. Soon afterward, he moved to Fort Smith, Arkansas where his oldest son had migrated some years prior.

## Settlers Trickle In 43

*Corn planted between girdled trees on Appalachian ridge (above). Quill Rose, noted moonshiner (left). Tub Mill on Sugar Fork (below).*

*Chapter 4*
# Subterranean Smokies

In the mid-1880's, across the river from Welch Cove on Little Fork Ridge in the Hazel Creek watershed, Fonzie Hall found something that would signal the beginning of an amazing cycle of changes that would transform the Fontana area from the frontier era to the forefront of American technology in a matter of decades. This rapid evolution—which had taken America in general about 200 years to accomplish—must have been quite a spectacle to the residents of the region.

Many of the speculators who had purchased large tracts of land after the Treaty of 1819 and the removal of the Cherokees in 1838 had hopes of financial gain from the exploitation of the natural resources such as minerals and timber. But by the late 1880's the area was virtually untouched other than by the pioneer farmsteads that dotted the valley land. The only town worthy of the name was Bryson City on the eastern end of the region.

By 1945, however, the Fontana area had yielded such quantities of natural resources in the form of minerals, timber, and water power that it could arguably rival any comparably-sized area in America. The efforts by the industrialists to remove, harvest, harness, and transport these resources were simultaneous and often co-dependant. The ferocity with which the legion of engineers, administrators, and workers pursued their goals was almost like waging war against the very land itself.

Fonzie Hall had travelled from his home at Webster, North

Carolina to visit his brother Crate who lived on Bone Valley Creek, a tributary of Hazel Creek. While there, Fonzie went off to do a little prospecting for mica. Mica is a sheetlike, translucent material found throughout the southern mountains that was used extensively for lamp chimneys, lamp shades, and even windows for buildings. As Fonzie walked along Little Fork Ridge he spotted a rock outcrop and broke off a piece with his pick ax. The inside of the rock was yellow and seemed metallic. Fonzie was sure he had found gold. He disguised the rock outcrop and set out for Crate's house. The brothers decided to keep the find secret—but they had to confirm it was gold. They took the specimen to a trusted neighbor, Bent Cook, who had experience in mineral identification. Cook recognized the yellow rock and pronounced to the disappointed brothers that it was copper. Copper was selling for only about eight and one-half cents a pound, making development of the remote find economically unfeasible at the time.

**Mouth of Adams-Westfeldt Mine, Sugar Fork of Hazel Creek.**

Crate Hall determined that the land where the copper was found belonged to Ep Everett, a land speculator who had been the sheriff and mayor of Bryson City. A few years later the price of copper had increased significantly and so had interest in copper deposits. A New York mineral developer, W.S. Adams, who had developed a kaolin clay deposit near Webster, found out about the Little Fork Ridge copper strike. Adams asked Mark Bryson, a local prospector, to secure an ore sample from the strike. Upon receiving the results of the assay of the ore, Adams promptly headed for Hazel Creek. (The average assay of ore from the large copper development at Copperhill, Tennessee was .02% copper; average assay of ore from the Fontana mine was 7%; and the average assay of ore from the Adams-Westfeldt mine was 32% copper).

Adams inspected the site, bought 200 acres from Ep Everett,

and began developing the mine. About a half-dozen dwelling houses, a bunk house, a cookhouse, shops, and a powder house were constructed. Several shallow shafts were sunk and before long the extremely rich ore was ready for shipment. That part of the plan however, presented problems. The closest railhead was at Bushnell, about 20 miles from the mine. Roads were improved to accommodate heavy ore wagons, but shipping raw ore by wagon was not economically feasible in the long run. Therefore, Adams planned to construct a crude open heap roaster at the hamlet of Medlin near the confluence of Sugar Fork and Hazel Creek.

Open heap roasting was basically a process where alternating layers of firewood and ore were placed to construct a heap or pile. The pile was then set afire. As the ore roasted, certain undesirable elements of the ore were burned off, thus concentrating the ore for shipment to the smelter. This method of copper processing is devastating to the environment in the vicinity of the roaster. First, the process required tremendous amounts of firewood, resulting in consumption of nearby forests. Next, the burning process released gaseous sulfuric acid. The gaseous acid is heavier than air, sinks to the ground, and kills all vegetation it contacts. Although mostly reforested today, many square miles of land around the roasters at Copperhill, Tennessee were completely denuded of all vegetation and resembled the moon.

Fortunately for the Hazel Creek watershed—but unfortunately for Mr. Adams—George Westfeldt entered the story in late 1900

**Adams-Westfeldt Copper Mine, Hazel Creek.**

**Adams-Westfeldt mine offices at Medlin, NC.**

just prior to the construction of the roaster. In 1869, Westfeldt, a New Orleans financier and land speculator, had purchased several tracts of land on Hazel Creek. At the time of this purchase, he had some difficulty locating the boundaries of his new property. Legal land descriptions of the day used wording such as "following the meander of the ridge" as boundary lines and "a red oak stump" as corners. In 1901, Westfeldt, convinced that he was the legal owner of the mine site, brought suit against Adams and stopped operations at the mine.

The dispute between Adams and Westfeldt over the ownership of the mine became the longest court case in the history of the United States. When one side would win a decision, the other side would appeal. Both sides accused the other of tampering with boundary line markings and many local people became involved in the dispute. Hazel Creek resident Granville Calhoun recalled years later seeing 22 lawyers, 11 for each side, in the courtroom at once. Each side spent about a quarter million dollars preparing and presenting their case. W.S. Adams and George

Westfeldt both died before the case was resolved. Finally, in 1927, 26 years after litigation had begun, a compromise was reached with the Adams heirs in control of the mine although the Westfeldt heirs retained a large interest in the property.

Due to the Great Depression and a general lack of interest on behalf of the heirs, the mine was not immediately reopened. It was eventually sold to the Kalb family of New York. Ironically, the window of time when W.M. Ritter's logging railroad was "just down the hill" from the mine had been missed due to the litigation. Therefore, when the Kalbs reopened operations in 1942 to help fulfill the wartime demand for copper, they had to truck the ore to the railhead at the mouth of Hazel Creek. The ore from this mine was so rich that even with the trucking expense, the Kalb's efforts were probably financially rewarding.

I have visited the mine site several times and today rocks still litter the site that are tarnished green on the outside like the Statue of Liberty, and when broken open reveal yellow raw copper. After only about 18 months of operation, the Kalbs were forced to sell the property to the Tennessee Valley Authority (TVA) as a result of construction of Fontana Dam and subsequent flooding of access to the Hazel Creek watershed. The property was later transferred to the Department of Interior and is now part of the Great Smoky Mountains National Park.

The copper strike on Little Fork Ridge was not an isolated mineral occurrence. Geologists have identified a strip of land running from the vicinity of Copperhill, Tennessee to the vicinity of Silers Bald, at the head of Hazel Creek, that holds a high possibility of yielding copper and other minerals. Jack Prince, Sr., local resident and one of the original surveyors for Fontana Dam, stated in an interview in 1986 that "TVA made a bad mistake in where they put Fontana Dam. They brought it right slap over this copper vein that goes through here to Copperhill, Tennessee. They came in here with the diamond drill crew. They drilled straight down in the bottom. That hole went back to about 480 feet and golly bum, they went through copper, copper, copper—150 to 200 feet of it, and it's still down there." Mining companies still have interest in the area. In 1995, B.H.P. Minerals International Exploration, Inc. applied for prospecting permits on national forest lands in the Fontana area.

Even though no sustained effort was ever made to develop

the ore body at the Adams-Westfeldt Mine, more copper ore was mined at the Fontana Mine, on the Eagle Creek Discovery, than at any place in North Carolina. In the early-1900's, George and R.E. Wood purchased large tracts of land on Eagle Creek to support operations of their Montvale Lumber Company's operations at that location. The name of the discoverer of the copper strike is not certain, family stories suggest that Dilly Welch, who lived for awhile on Ecoah Branch, found it. A Dr. Post, who lived in Cades Cove, spent a great deal of time prospecting for minerals, and about 1850 made a map showing deposits on Eagle Creek. Or it could have been an employee of Montvale Lumber Company who followed the mineral stained waters of a small spring branch to the copper bearing outcrop just off Ecoah Branch, a tributary of Eagle Creek. In 1926, Dr. J.F. Riter, along with several other investors, formed the Fontana Mining Corporation, which was affiliated with the Ducktown Chemical and Iron Company that had mines and a smelter at Isabella, Tennessee. The Fontana Mining Corporation leased the mine site from Montvale Lumber Company and commenced operations.

**Fontana mine camp on Ecoah Branch of Eagle Creek**

C.F. SEAMAN

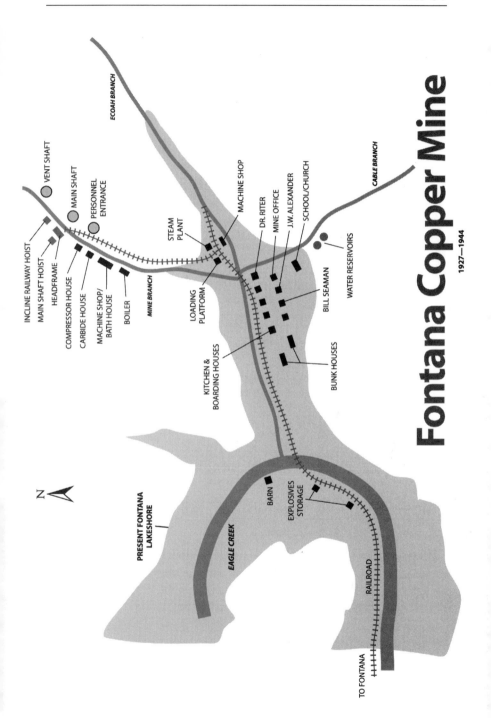

**Fontana Copper Mine and headframe.**

Just as at the Adams-Westfeldt Mine, the first step was to construct housing and support facilities near the mine site. Unlike the Adams-Westfeldt, Montvale Lumber Company's narrow gauge railroad ran along Eagle Creek less than one half mile from the mine entrance. A narrow gauge spurline was built up Ecoah Branch and a compact mining village was constructed along the spur. Residences for Dr. Riter, J.W. Alexander, the mine superintendent, Mr. Seamen, the civil engineer, and a large combination cookhouse-bunkhouse were some of the first buildings constructed. A concrete springhouse or cold storage area was built into the basement of the cookhouse and can be seen today when Fontana Lake is drawn down in winter. This building was later converted to a residence and occupied by Rob Mull and later Arthur Watkins.

A machine shop, boiler house, compressor house, and ore handling area were built at the upper end of the village cove. Up at the mine entrance, hoisting and loading equipment was installed. As time passed, a combination school-church-theater, additional residences and bunkhouses were also built. Montvale Lumber Company's operations on Eagle Creek were completed by late 1927. This resulted in the availability of vacated facilities at their company town of Fontana, located at the confluence of Eagle Creek and the Little T., for use by the mining company.

The mine itself consisted of a curving, near-vertical main shaft driven to a depth of 2,150 feet below the surface. Later a straight, vertical shaft replaced the old curving one to facilitate better operations of lifting equipment. At about 100 foot intervals as the shaft descended, lateral tunnels or levels were excavated that followed the ore body lenses. The Fontana Mine had 20 levels. The ore was excavated from these lateral levels, called stopes. Pillars of ore were left unexcavated in the stopes to support the roof of the resulting chamber. Some of the stopes were quite cavernous.

When approaching the Fontana Mine today, the visitor will find three large holes in the ground surrounded by chain link fencing. The first hole, as one ascends the branch leading to the mine, is actually the end of the first mine level. This was the personnel entrance to the mine. The miners would simply walk through this level and catch the lift that was hoisted up and down the main shaft to the level of the work. Once at work, the miners would bore holes with jack hammers operated at first by steam, then later by compressed air into the ore body face. These holes would then be loaded with explosives and detonated. The ore would fall to the floor of the stope where it was loaded into skip cars that were hoisted via the main shaft back to the surface. By 1931, a 191,000 volt electric line had been constructed from the Rymers Ferry Power House to help power the mine operations.

*Fontana Mine hoist, awaiting the return of the miners.*

The second hole the visitor encounters while ascending the mine branch is the mouth of the main shaft. The head frame and tipple, a device to unload the skip cars by tipping them and dumping their load into narrow gauge ore cars positioned beneath, was located in the floor of the narrow valley adjacent to the main shaft opening. A large drum-type steam winch supplied by the S. Flory Manufacturing Company of Bangor, Pennsylvania is still in place across from the main shaft opening. This winch was the motive power for the main shaft lift.

The third hole, just up from the main shaft opening, was a ventilation shaft for a blacksmith shop located on the first level across from the personnel entrance. This ingenious arrangement meant that drilling steel to be sharpened and other equipment to be repaired did not have to be transported outside the mine. In addition, the chamber on the first level provided a ready-made, climate-controlled shop space. The ventilation shaft opening is still soot stained from the blacksmith fires below.

A second smaller winch was secured to a massive concrete anchor just uphill from the base of the tipple. This winch was used to raise and lower the narrow gauge ore cars on a steeply inclined railway from the village to the mine. A railway switchyard was located at the mine village that allowed the loaded ore cars to be consolidated into trains which were pulled to the ore dump at the Carolina and Tennessee Southern Railway tracks at Fontana. These ore trains were at first pulled by two dinkey locomotives. The

**Ore dump and bridge at Fontana, N.C. — the western terminus of the Carolina and Tennessee Southern Railroad.**

C.F. SEAMAN

dinkeys were soon replaced by a powerful Shay geared locomotive. At first the ore was transferred from the narrow gauge ore cars to standard gauge ore cars by hand. Later a tipple device was installed that actually dumped the contents from the smaller narrow gauge car to the larger standard gauge cars. The ore was then shipped by rail to the smelter in Isabella, Tennessee for processing.

The fact that the Fontana Mine ore was shipped such a great distance is a testimony to its richness. From March 1926 through the mine closure on January 31, 1944, 584,350 tons of ore were shipped that produced over 85,000,000 pounds of copper. Several people I have interviewed over the years about the mine have stated that "The copper was just a by-product of the mine—gold and silver were really what the company was after." It was common practice for mining companies of the day not to list gold and silver content on published assays. Examination of the Fontana Mine records at the Ducktown Basin Museum in Ducktown, Tennessee show this was the practice at the Fontana Mine while operated by the Fontana Mining Corporation.

On February 1, 1931, the mine was purchased from Montvale Lumber Company by the North Carolina Exploration Company, an affiliate of Tennessee Copper and Chemical Company that was later acquired by the Cities Services Realty Corporation. Operations and personnel at the mine were little effected by the change of ownership. Examination of Cities Services' records reveals that assay quantities of gold and silver were published after 1931 and that efforts were made at the smelter to recover these minerals along with zinc, sulfur, and iron. Records show that between February 1931 and July 1942 the ore shipped from the Fontana Mine contained 0.0072 oz./ton of gold and 0.385 oz./ton of silver. During this period, 251,224 tons of ore were shipped. Simple mathematics reveal that between 1931 and 1942 the potential existed for the recovery of 1,808.8 ounces of gold and 96,721.2 ounces of silver from the ore from the Fontana Mine.

Production at the mine varied with a number of factors, not the least of which was the national economy. Not long after the North Carolina Exploration Company bought the mine, the effects of the Great Depression were felt. Employment dropped from over 300 to less than 50. The main shaft had been driven to the 15th level (about 1,500 feet deep) by 1931, the 17th level by 1935, and

C.F. SEAMAN

*Fontana copper mine camp, 1930.*

20th level by 1939.

    By mid-1943, mine management had realized the impending loss of access to the mine due to the construction of Fontana Lake. For several years prior, high war time demand had resulted in a rob and retreat approach to ore removal. High grade pillars of ore were removed from the lower levels and those levels were allowed to flood. A deep-shaft mine is like a large water well; therefore, continual pumping is required to keep the mine dry. A detailed report on the ore reserves at the Fontana Mine by geologist Dr. W.H. Emmons dated August 1942 and a July 10, 1943, letter from mine superintendent J.W. Alexander to Dr. Emmons indicates that the mine was flooded to the 8th level. And that exploration and examination indicated that a considerable ore body remained unexcavated in the mine. A search of retired Fontana mining records by Cities Services in 1975 concluded that the remaining probable, and possible ore body at the Fontana Mine had a gross value of 19.7 million dollars.

    Even though all other land owners between the Little Tennessee River and the existing Great Smoky Mountains National Park boundary were forced to sell their land to TVA for inclusion in the park, Cities Services was allowed to retain title to the 2,343 acre mine property. In 1972 the National Park Service conducted several studies to establish the practicality of reopening the mine. In his evaluation of the Fontana Mine, dated April 14, 1972, National Park Service mining engineer Robert D. O'Brien concluded: "The Fontana Mine is owned by the North Carolina Exploration Co. which is a subsidiary of the Tennessee Corporation. The operation of the Fontana Mine during the period of 1931 to 1942 was a losing operation for seven years out of the twelve years. According to Federal income tax statements from the files of the Tennessee Valley Authority, the operation had a net loss of $151,743 over twelve years. I am sure that if the Tennessee Corporation was in need of the ore from the Fontana Mine to continue the operations of the smelter at Isabella, Tennessee that they could afford to operate at a loss. It does not seem reasonable to me, however, that they would submit to a loss of over $2,000,000 in a seven year period. This would be more than a paper loss. On the basis of the present small ore body; the unfavorable geological prospects for any additional ore bodies; and the projected loss of money from an anticipated operation I can see no reason to value the mine at any more than the present land value."

Then in a report dated May 8, 1972, Phillip O. Stewart, Chief, Division of Land Acquisition for the National Park Service surmised "At this time there does not appear to be any alternative to the action of acquiring the property and prohibiting mining and related activities. Practical and economic aspects of resuming mining operations does not offer a promising return on investment. If the Cities Services Realty Corporation decides not to mine the deposit but still retains the title there is an adverse effect upon the Great Smoky National Park which is apparent now and could become worse. The National Park is closed to hunting but hunters approach the Park through the private lands. Since the boundary is irregular and not well marked it is difficult to ascertain where the game is taken. This constitutes a nuisance to the Park Management which could increase."

The National Park Service purchased the Fontana Mine property from Cities Services Realty Corporation in 1983 for about one million dollars and the property was added to the Great Smoky Mountains National Park.

*Chapter 5*
# The Race Begins

**U**tilization of forest products in the Fontana area, like all of the southern Appalachians, began when the first Native Americans wandered into the region thousands of years ago. Fruits and nuts were harvested for food, trees were cut for firewood, lodging and canoes, and later on fields were cleared for agriculture. Timberstand management techniques were even practiced by the Indians in the form of burning forest undergrowth to create an open type forest that facilitated hunting. But by and large, when the first white settlers came to the Fontana area around 1800, they were entering the forest primeval. These pioneer settlers first felled trees to build cabins and farm buildings. Soon they began enlarging the old Indian fields they found along the watercourses and clearing "new ground" to fulfill their agricultural needs. After the Civil War, a few water powered grist mills were fitted with sawmill equipment and very limited commercial lumber operations were started by local inhabitants. Even so, by the 1880's the great timber resources of the area were still virtually untouched.

A tremendous lumber industry was in full swing in the United States by the late 1800's and had consumed huge forests throughout the South, East, and North. The first large commercial timber operations to penetrate the fastness of the Smokies—particularly the Fontana area—were Taylor & Crate, Loomis & Wheeler, W.C. Heyser & Co., and others. These early loggers found vast tracts of magnificent virgin timber, but they faced the same problem that hampered all early resource development—transportation.

In other parts of the country and even in the lower elevations of the Appalachians, floating logs down rivers to the sawmill was the accepted method to transport timber. The Little Tennessee River had sufficient water flow to free float logs under most conditions, but even the larger tributary streams such as Hazel Creek did not. The lumbermen devised a method to increase the flow in these streams and move their logs called splash dams. Crude log dams were built at strategic points along a creek or small river. Some were more sophisticated, with gates that could be opened and closed, while others were simply blown up with explosives to release their load of water and logs. Three of the more sophisticated types were built along Hazel Creek. Streambeds were often cleared of large boulders and other obstructions to facilitate the float. Only the best trees, which were growing reasonably close to the stream, and that would float such as poplar, basswood, cucumber, and white pine, were cut into log lengths. The logs' ends would be somewhat rounded so they would glance off obstructions. Each log was then branded with the lumber company's mark so the owner could be identified when they reached the log boom or sawmill. The logs were then skidded by oxen or horses into the streambed or the pond behind the splash dam. When the "system" was loaded, the loggers would wait for a freshet or rainy period when the flow in the stream was as high as possible. The uppermost dam would then be opened and the flood of water and logs would start downstream, picking up other logs as it went. Just as the flood reached the next dam, it was opened, multiplying the size and force of the tumult as it hurtled downstream. Loggers called river hogs or drivers, equipped with caulked or spiked boots and pike poles, followed and sometimes

**The mighty chestnut.**

**Splash Dam.**

rode down on the flood to dislodge snags and break up jams.

A log boom was installed by the Babcock Boom & Lumber Company at Chillhowee where the Little T. leaves the mountains and enters the flatland of the Tennessee Valley. The log boom was constructed by attaching a string of very buoyant logs end to end with chains and stretching them across the river. As the free floating logs came down the river they would be caught behind the boom. The river hogs could then bind each company's logs into rafts that were floated to the sawmills at Chattanooga, Tennessee.

These early logging companies, and later the big lumber companies that moved into the area, usually bought only what land was needed to build the improvements needed for their operations. Agents for the various companies would execute legal agreements with land owners and purchase their timber. These agreements were quite specific and were often recorded with the Register of Deeds in the county in which the transaction took place. Examination of a couple of these agreements made by our friend Jessie Gunter reveals much about how the system worked. An agreement registered on May 19th, 1885 states:

> For and in consideration of the sum of ($115.05) one hundred and fifteen dollars and five cents paid to us by J.F. Loomis & Xebaphon Wheeler of Chattanooga, Tennessee, the receipt of which is hereby acknowledged. We J.C. Gunter and A.C. Gunter his wife of Graham County, North Carolina, have bargained and sold and do by these presents grant, bargain, sell, transfer and convey unto the said J.F. Loomis & Xenaphon Wheeler (318) three hundred and eighteen poplar, ash, Yellow cucumber, pine, white walnut & (46) forty six white pine two feet and over in diameter at the butt, situated on our land in Graham County on the waters of the Tennessee River, in District No. 10, covered by grant 2577 tract No. 629, and grant N. 2075 and grant N. 2069 and Entry No. 357.

The rights of the purchaser were pretty clearly spelled out:

**Snaking logs with a six-ox team.**

> Which poplar, ash, cucumber, walnut and pine trees are marked with the letter L ell. Said J.F. Loomis & Xenaphon Wheeler or their heirs and assigns shall have the right to enter upon the lands upon which said trees are situated and upon any other lands belonging to us, for the purpose of cutting and removing said trees whenever they may so desire, and shall have the right of ingress and egress over the same, and the right to make such roads over any of said lands suitable and proper to enable them to remove said trees whenever they may so desire and we further agree with the parties of the first part, that we will not do anything or cause anything to be done to injure or kill said trees. We covenant with the said J.F. Loomis & Xenaphon Wheeler, their heirs and assigns that we are lawfully seized of said trees, and have good right to sell and convey the same, that they are unincumbered and further that we will forever warrant and defend the title to the same against the Lawful claims of all persons whomsoever. As witness our

hands and seals, on this the 5th day of May A.D. 1885.

Then in an agreement dated August 28, 1888, Jessie Gunter was actually contracted to cut and deliver the trees he sold in the first agreement along with trees sold by some of his neighbors:

*This Agreement made this 28th day of August 1888, between J.C. Gunter of Graham County, N.C. and W.C. Heyser & Co. of Chattanooga, Tenn. Witnesseth: That said J.C. Gunter agrees to cut down all the trees purchased by Loomis & Wheeler of James Turner, P.C. Gunter, Z.V. Gunter and J.C. Gunter in Graham County, N.C. Said trees are to be cut into logs by said W.C. Heyser & Co. or their agent and it is understood and agreed that no odd feet will be counted in measuring and all logs shall have an excess of four (4) inches in length that shall not be counted in the measurement. Said Gunter agrees to cut the trees as carefully as possible so as to injure or destroy as little timber as possible. Said logs shall be by said Gunter delivered to W.C. Heyser & Co. in the Tennessee River and it is understood and agreed that all the logs are to be peeled of their bark before delivering into said River, and said Gunter agrees to employ every reasonable means to deliver said timber as soon as possible and it is understood that all of the timber is to be delivered in two (2) years from the date of this instrument. But at the expiration of the time, should said Gunter fail to deliver all of said timber it is understood that the time will be extended six (6) months provided said Gunter has been faithfully in his endeavors to comply with his contract for the logs as delivered. Said W.C. Heyser & Co. agree to pay said J.C. Gunter at the rate of $4.25 per thousand feet board measure according to Scrihners rules paying of said sum 2/3 as the logs are put into the river and retaining the remaining 1/3 until the contract is fully completed. But at the end of the first year if said J.C. Gunter can show that the timber he has delivered is on equal diversion of the expense of moving the timber and delivering the same into the river from the entire tract of land, included in this contract, then said W.C. Heyser & Co. are to give said Gunter a Settlement in full for all timber delivered. They also Engage to have the Logs put on the bank of the river, measured at least twice every month and that 2/3 of the contract price shall be paid about the 1st and 15th of each month.*

The activity by these early logging companies just scratched the edges of the vast forest reserve in the Fontana area. Just a few

**Horace Kephart in his cabin on Hazel Creek.**

years into the 20th century things would change drastically. Horace Kephart, a librarian by training, states in Chapter One of his wonderful book *Our Southern Highlanders* first published in 1913:

> The Southern highlands themselves are a mysterious realm. When I prepared, in 1904, for my first sojourn in the Great Smoky Mountains, which form the master chain of the Appalachian system, I could find in no library a guide to that region. The most diligent research failed to discover so much as a magazine article, written within this generation, that described the land and its people. Nay, there was not even a novel or a story that showed intimate local knowledge. Had I been going to Teneriffe or Timbuctu, the libraries would have furnished information a-plenty; but about this housetop of eastern America they were strangely silent; it was terra incognita.
> 
> On the map I could see that the Southern Appalachians cover an area much larger than New England, and that they are nearer the center of our population than any other mountains that deserve the name.

# The Race Begins 65

*Why, then, so little known? Quaintly there came to mind those lines familiar to my boyhood: 'Get you up this way southward, and go up into the mountain; and see the land, what it is; and the people that dwelleth therein, whether they be strong or weak, few or many; and what the land is that they dwell in, whether it be good or bad; and what cities they be that they dwell in, whether in tents, or in strongholds; and what the land is, whether it be fat or lean, whether there be wood therein or not.' In that dustiest room of a great library where 'pub.docs.' are stored, I unearthed a government report on forestry that gave, at last, a clear idea of the lay of the land.*

Ironically the public document Kephart referred to, although intended to be a plea to establish a vast national forest reserve in the southern Appalachians, could be viewed as an elaborate advertisement to America's lumbermen detailing the tremendous wealth of timber contained in the region.

The "pub.doc." in question was the *Report on the Forests and Forest Conditions of the Southern Appalachian Mountain Region*. Prepared by the Secretary of Agriculture in collaboration with the Department of the Interior, the report was the direct result of a proposal that the government protect the Appalachian forests by purchasing the land and making it a great national forest reserve. The concept was first brought directly to the attention of Congress in January, 1900, when a memorial to that effect was presented by the Appalachian Mountain Club of New England and the Appalachian National Park Association of the South Atlantic States.

**Horse drawn log wagon.**

In response to this memorial and in recognition of the importance of the movement, the act making the appropriation for the Department of Agriculture for the fiscal year ending June 30, 1901, provided that a "sum not to exceed $5,000 may, in the discretion of the Secretary of Agriculture, be used to investigate the forest conditions in the southern Appalachian mountain region of western North Carolina and adjacent states." The Secretary of Agriculture, James Wilson, described the effects of the timber companies as follows:

> The lumberman attacked this forest several decades ago when he began to penetrate it in search of the rarer and more valuable trees, such as the walnut and cherry. Later, as the railroads entered the region to some extent, he added to his list of trees for cutting the mountain birch, locust, and tulip poplar, and successively other valuable species. During the past few years he has cut everything merchantable. He is now beginning to extend his operations to considerable distances beyond the main lines of transportation by the construction of tramways and even cheap, short railways. Meanwhile his search for the more valuable trees has extended in advance to most of the more remote mountain coves.
>
> In these operations there has naturally been no thought for the future. Trees have been cut so as to fall along the line of least resistance regardless of what they crush. Their tops and branches, instead of being piled in such way and burned at such time as would do the least harm, are left scattered among the adjacent growth to burn when driest, and thus destroy or injure everything within reach. The home and permanent interests of the lumberman are generally in another State or region, and his interest in these mountains begins and ends with the hope of profit. There is, however, no evidence that the native lumberman has in the past exhibited any different spirit.

**Logged over area.**

President Theodore Roosevelt listed the Secretary of Agriculture's conclusions in his December 19, 1901, Letter of Transmittal of the report to the Senate and House of Representatives. Those conclusions were as follows:

1) The Southern Appalachian region embraces the highest peaks and largest mountain masses east of the Rockies. It is the great physiographic feature of the eastern half of the continent, and no such lofty mountains are covered with hard-wood forests in all North America.

2) Upon these mountains descends the heaviest rainfall of the United States, except that of the North Pacific coast. It is often of extreme violence, as much as 8 inches having fallen in eleven hours, 31 inches in one month, and 105 inches in a year.

3) The soil, once denuded of its forests and swept by torrential rains, rapidly loses first its humus, then its rich upper strata, and finally is washed in enormous volume into the streams, to bury much of the fertile lowlands as are not eroded by the floods, to obstruct the rivers, and to fill up the harbors on the coast. More good soil is now washed from these cleared mountain-side fields during a single heavy rain than during centuries under forest cover.

4) The rivers which originate in the Southern Appalachians flow into or along the edges of every State from Ohio to the Gulf and from the Atlantic to the Mississippi. Along their courses are agricultural, waterpower, and navigation interests whose preservation is absolutely essential to the well-being of the nation.

5) The regulation of the flow of these rivers can be accomplished only by the conservation of the forests.

6) These are the heaviest and most beautiful hard-wood forests of the continent. In them species from east and west, from north and south, mingle in a growth of unparalleled richness and variety. They contain many species of the first commercial value, and furnish important supplies which can not be obtained from any other region.

7) For economic reasons the preservation of these forests is imperative. Their existence in good condition is essential to the prosperity of the lowlands through which their waters run. Maintained in productive condition they will supply indispensable materials, which must fail without them. Their management under practical and conservative forestry will sustain and increase the resources of this region and of the nation at large, will serve as an invaluable object lesson in the advantages and

**Nantahala Gorge around the turn of the century.**

practicability of forest preservation by use, and will soon be self-supporting from the sale of timber.

8) The agricultural resources of the Southern Appalachian region must be protected and preserved. To that end the preservation of the forests is an indispensable condition, which will lead not to the reduction but to the increase of the yield of agricultural products.

9) The floods in these mountain-born streams, if this forest destruction continues, will increase in frequency and violence and in the extent of their damages, both within this region and across the bordering States. The extent of these damages, like those from the washing of the mountain fields and roads, can not be estimated with perfect accuracy, but during the present year alone the total has approximated $10,000,000, a sum sufficient to purchase the entire area recommended for the proposed reserve. But this loss can not be estimated in money value alone. Its continuance means the early destruction of conditions most valuable to the nation, and which neither skill nor wealth can restore.

10) The preservation of the forests, of the streams, and of the agricul-

tural interests here described can be successfully accomplished only by the purchase and creation of a national forest reserve. The States of the Southern Appalachian region own little or no land, and their revenues are inadequate to carry out this plan. Federal action is obviously necessary, is fully justified by reasons of public necessity, and may be expected to have most fortunate results.

At the end of his Letter of Transmittal, Theodore Roosevelt wrote that "With these conclusions I fully agree; and I heartily commend this measure to the favorable consideration of the Congress."

The report included sections on "Forests and Forest Conditions in the Southern Appalachians"; "Lumbering in the Southern Appalachians"; "Description of the Southern Appalachian Forests, By River Basin"; and "Trees of the Southern Appalachians." Whether the report encouraged some lumbermen to move into the region quickly before the preservation movement gained a solid foothold is a matter for conjecture. But one thing is for certain, the timing was perfect. Within just a few years, five very large and very sophisticated lumber companies descended on the Fontana area. The first challenge facing the newly arrived lumber barons was the old nemesis—transportation. However, these boys had a plan—railroads.

*Chapter 6*

# Mountain Rails

The first thoughts of a railroad into western North Carolina probably occurred in the late 1700's when the first residents heard of the wooden rail tramways pulled by horses that were being installed in England, Canada, and the northeastern United States. In the 1820's an English inventor, Robert Stephenson, adapted Thomas Watt's steam engine to a wheeled vehicle and created the steam locomotive. In the early 1830's Baltimore merchant Peter Cooper produced the first American locomotive, the "Tom Thumb," and initiated a technology that would change America forever. The decades that followed saw an explosion of railroads and railroad equipment. Railroad mileage in the United States multiplied rapidly: by 1840—2,500 miles; by 1850—9,000 miles; and by 1860 over 25,000 miles of track had been constructed.

Soon after railroad technology emerged, southern leaders such as John C. Calhoun, Dr. John Caldwell, Joel Poinsett, Colonel William H. Thomas, and others envisioned a railroad from the coastal ports of Charleston and Beaufort to Tennessee and the agriculturally rich Mississippi Valley. The most direct route would have taken this road across the southern Appalachians. The fact that the poor roads of the region were dangerously inadequate was illustrated by a crop failure in western North Carolina in 1845 that created famine-like conditions for residents in the mountains, while the Tennessee Valley and coastal Carolina were enjoying bumper crops. Concerted pressure from the region's citizens, coupled with the old vision "of constructing a railroad to effect a communication between the North Carolina Railroad and the Valley of the Mississippi," resulted in the 1855 charter of the

***Railroad building crew.***

Western North Carolina Railroad from Salisbury on the North Carolina Railroad to near Asheville by the North Carolina State Legislature. In 1859 the charter was amended to continue the line from Asheville "extending west through the valley of the Pigeon and Tuckasegee Rivers to a point on the line of the Blue Ridge Railroad on the (Little) Tennessee River, or to the Tennessee state line at or near Ducktown in the county of Cherokee." The legislation also "provided that the extension from Asheville might be down the French Broad River, through Madison County, to the line of the state of Tennessee at or near Paint Rock, which might connect with any company that has been formed or may be formed to complete the railroad connection with the East Tennessee and Virginia Railroad."

The Blue Ridge Railroad—or the Carolina and Tennessee Southern, as a part of it was later known—was first chartered in 1851 by four companies in four states. This route, also conceived to be a main line connection from the southern coastal ports to the fertile Midwest, was to run from Anderson, South Carolina via Walhalla, South Carolina to Clayton, Georgia and the headwaters of the Little Tennessee River, and then follow the Little T. past Franklin, North Carolina through the heart of what would become the Fontana area on to Maryville and Knoxville, Tennessee. Although much planning, posturing, and legislation had been completed on these railroads, only about 20 miles of the Western North Carolina from Salisbury to near Morganton and 34 miles of the Blue Ridge from Anderson to Walhalla had been constructed prior to a complete shutdown due to the onset of the Civil War in 1861.

After the war, very little progress was made on the Blue Ridge Line other than two short disconnected sections that will be discussed later. The Western North Carolina Railroad, on the other hand, seemed destined to become a reality. The line would survive through tenacious efforts of organization, construction, and administration through the present day. Soon after the end of the war, the WNCRR was completed to Old Fort in 1869 at the foot of the Blue Ridge Mountains. At this point the railway faced many daunting challenges, not the least of which was construction of

**Wooden railroad trestle.**

COURTESY OF GSMNP

COURTESY OF GSMNP

**Railroads finally penetrate the mountain fastness.**

the tracks up Old Fort Mountain toward Asheville. The next seven years saw a tangled series of legal and financial maneuvers that would have surely killed other similar projects. Ownership of the railroad changed several times during this period; even the state of North Carolina owned the line for a time. Ironically, this would not be the only time state government would step in to preserve the future of this railroad.

Although never caught or convicted, two accused swindlers, George Swepson and Milton Littlefield, added to the intrigue of the period. The incident reportedly involved a daring midnight escape in a darkened locomotive. The exact circumstances are complicated, involving numerous politicians, but the fact remained that Littlefield and $4,000,000 in state issued railroad bonds were never seen again.

Convict labor was pressed into service to build the line and hundreds lost their lives in the dangerous work, including 19 inmates that were chained together when their boat overturned in the raging floodwaters of the Tuckasegee River while crossing to work on the Cowee Tunnel. Their bodies were found still chained in a lump on the bottom of the river and it is said that the tunnel is haunted. Indeed, several accidents and cave-ins have occurred at the tunnel. Incorrect surveys, landslides, relocations, and extremely steep grades all plagued the builders.

Despite all the hardships, the tracks were completed to Asheville in 1880. After reaching Asheville, W.J. Best & Company, owners of the railroad at that time, put their primary efforts into completion of the line down the French Broad River and reached Paint Rock, near the Tennessee state line, in late 1882. This line operated today by Northfork Southern would become the long dreamed of main line connection across the southern Appalachians. Emphasis then shifted to complete the western line which would become known as the Murphy Branch. The tracks reached Bryson City in early 1884 and were continued down the Tuckasegee River to the town of Bushnell, then up the Little T. to

**Early train wrecks were common.**

OLIVER COLLECTION

the Nantahala River and the community of Nantahala at the base of Red Marble Mountain by the end of 1884. Finally the east end of the Fontana area had a rail connection to the east.

Major difficulty was encountered trying to push the tracks through Red Marble Gap at Topton, but eventually the tracks reached Andrews in mid-1889 and the town of Murphy in 1891, 34 years after construction had begun. The Murphy Branch connected with the Georgia and North Carolina Railroad, which had reached Murphy in 1888, providing a southerly connection for the line. This would be the route later taken by thousands of ore cars from the Fontana Mine on their way to the smelter at Isabella, Tennessee.

Only three years after reaching Murphy, the Richmond and

**Steam train heading into the Nantahala Gorge near Topton.**

Danville Railroad Company, the last in a long string of owners of the line during the construction years, lost control of the Murphy Branch to the Southern Railway Company. Southern would reap the harvest on the Murphy Branch during its glory years. Passengers, agricultural goods, logs and lumber, copper ore, and thousands of tons of construction materials would make the Murphy a very busy branch line from 1894 through 1946. The Murphy Branch would fall on hard time as did so many railroads in America, but—as we shall see—the tenacious little line would survive and even prosper.

Chapter 7
# The Back of Beyond Booms

**M**eanwhile, back at the turn of the century, the lumber barons were planning their attack on the vast forests of the Fontana area. The first thing to do was for the various companies to stake their claim on the different watersheds. No documentation can be found to substantiate the fact, but there must have been some cooperation between the companies. It was economically and operationally vital for a company to control the timber rights in the vicinity of its sawmill, usually a watershed. One might imagine expensively dressed tycoons huddled in a smoky office car on a railroad side track drawing lines on a map; or maybe timber buying agents interacting in the field and making recommendations to their bosses; or some sort of understood pecking order; or just a first-come first-claim system.

Whatever method was used, the results were pretty impressive. Norwood Lumber Company would log Forney Creek, W.M. Ritter Lumber Company would log Hazel Creek, Montvale Lumber Company took Eagle Creek, Kitchens Lumber Company was on Twenty Mile Creek, and Whiting Manufacturing Company would log most of the south or Graham County side of the river. Of course the division of territory was not ironclad. There was some overlap between the big companies, and a number of smaller companies such as Buchanon Lumber Company, Graham County Lumber Company, Marvel Lumber Company, and Alarka Lumber Company all operated in the Fontana area.

After negotiating timber rights in the areas to be cut and purchasing what land was needed for all their support and manufacturing facilities, providing reliable transportation was the first order of business. This meant building railroads from the main line Murphy Branch to the various areas of operations. Standard gauge tracks would be required to run to each company's mills so that the finished lumber products could be loaded onto standard gauge box cars for delivery throughout the nation's rail system. Norwood would locate its main operations at the town of Forney, and Whiting at the town of Judson, both on the Murphy Branch, so only short standard gauge connections would be needed for them to start construction of facilities. Ritter, Montvale, and Kitchens would locate a considerable distance down the river and would require a branch line to be built down the river from Bushnell.

W.M. Ritter Company, the first and largest company to set up in the area, approached the Southern Railway Company concerning this work. Southern had acquired the Carolina and Tennessee Southern, part of the ill fated Blue Ridge Railway, who held the charter for a railroad along the Little Tennessee River. Realizing the freight potential, Southern agreed to build and operate 12 miles of standard gauge track from Bushnell to the mouth of Hazel Creek where Ritter Lumber Company would build the Ritter Station and a 15 car switch yard. Southern would later extend the line another two miles to Montvale's town of Fontana. These 17 miles of track would be the entire operation of the Carolina & Tennessee Southern Railroad. With the output of three large

**Town of Bushnell, junction of the Murphy Branch and the Carolina and Tennessee Southern Railroads.**

lumber operations, the Fontana copper mine ore shipments, and all the materials required to build Fontana Dam, the Carolina & Tennessee Southern could have arguably been the busiest 17 mile railroad in the country.

*Ritter Depot, located at the junction of the Carolina and Tennessee Southern and Ritter's Smoky Mountain Railroad.*

W.M. Ritter's decision to locate his mills and company town about three miles up Hazel Creek from the Carolina & Tennessee meant that a short standard gauge railway would have to be built to connect the two. For that purpose, the W.M. Ritter Lumber Company chartered the Smoky Mountain Railroad Company as an independent common carrier and constructed the line.

The steam locomotives that were used on the main lines of the day were called rod engines. Many of the rod engines used in the south were built by Baldwin Locomotive Works, H.K. Porter & Company, Cooke Locomotive & Machinery, and others. Rod engines are the classic steam locomotives immortalized in American folklore. They had at least one steam piston on each side placed in

*Ritter Lumber's Smoky Mountain RR passenger train, 1923.*

a horizontal position. The pistons operated pushrods that were attached directly to one edge of a counter balanced drive wheel. Rod engines were very efficient once at speed, but had definite traction and power disadvantages—particularly at slow speed. The steep grades, heavy loads, slow speeds, and sharp turns encountered on railroads used in the forest environment for the removal of logs proved extremely problematic for standard rod engines. A very first step in solving these problems was to narrow the gauge or distance between the tracks. This simply required less excavation and materials while building the tracks. Almost all logging railroads were narrow gauge.

**Graham County Railroad's "Sidewinder"—*a 70 ton, three piston Shay.***

HOLLAND COLLECTION

Ephraim Shay, a Michigan lumberman and inventor addressed the problem of logging with a locomotive and produced a marvelous solution—the geared locomotive. The steam pistons on a geared locomotive were placed so that their pushrods turned a crankshaft, much like in a modern internal combustion engine. This arrangement efficiently transformed the back-and-forth or up-and-down motion of the pushrods into the circular motion required to turn the wheels of the locomotive. This rotational energy could easily be transferred via driveshafts and gears to deliver very controllable power to the drive wheels. Further refinements would see not only drive wheels at the rear of the locomotive but also at the front, creating the forerunner of the modern four wheel drive. The drive wheels were grouped on independent carriage assemblies called trucks. The drive wheel trucks were made so that they could turn underneath the locomotive frame, allowing the geared locomotives to negotiate very sharp curves. With their tremendous power, all wheel drive, front and rear steering, and bulky design, I have always thought of geared logging locomotives as the predecessor of the modern monster truck. Wouldn't it be great to see a tail to tail tug of war between a 70-ton, three truck Shay and the 1,000 plus horsepower "Big Foot"? Gentlemen, start your engines!

Three primary manufacturers of geared locomotives emerged around the turn of the century. The Lima Locomotive Company in Lima, Ohio produced the well known and widely used Shay locomotives. Shays were commonly called Sidewinders. Their boilers were placed off center on the frame to provide space for two or three vertical pistons placed on the other side. The pistons turned a crankshaft that turned a driveshaft that ran conspicuously down one side of the locomotive.

The Hiesler Locomotive Company of Eerie, Pennsylvania produced Charles Hiesler's version of the geared locomotive. Hieslers had one piston on either side in a V-type arrangement that turned a crankshaft and subsequently a central driveshaft.

Climax Locomotives, manufactured by the Climax Manufacturing Company of Corry, Pennsylvania were a hybrid between a rod engine and geared locomotive. Their pistons, one on each side, were placed on an angle with their pushrods attached to one side of a counterweighted flywheel, much like a rod engine. The flywheel turned a driveshaft with power transferred to the drive

*Kitchen's Heisler #7 logging locomotive, factory photo.*

wheels via gears and driveshafts. Although Climax produced some very large and powerful locomotives, many of the Climax engines used in the Smokies were the small, economical Class "A" type with an upright boiler and wooden frame. All three brands and many configurations of geared locomotives were utilized by the companies logging the Fontana area.

Narrow gauge logging railroads were built by each company from their sawmill up the main creek in the watershed to be logged. Spur lines would be built up tributary streams. Main line railroads generally have maximum grades of about 3% with rare steep sections such as the Topton grade on the Murphy Branch approaching 5%. Narrow gauge logging railroads were commonly on grades of 10% and sometimes as steep as 14%. Often sand would be applied to the rails to keep the locomotives from spinning.

Some pretty amazing engineering feats were accomplished to conquer even steeper grades. A standard practice for running tracks up a mountainside was to use switchbacks. Tracks would be constructed in a zig-zag fash-

*Logging railroad switchback.*

COURTESY OF GSMNP

ion on a 10%—12% grade up the face of the mountain. Track switches would be placed at the intersection points and a dead end track long enough to accommodate the log train would be installed past the switches. The locomotive would pull the log train up the first section through the switch and out the dead end. The switch would then be thrown to allow passage to the next section and the locomotive would push or shove the train up the next section. Occasionally, incline tracks would be built straight up a mountain on grades as steep as 45%. A self-contained steam winch would be placed on the tracks at the bottom of the incline and its cable would be secured at the top. The winch could then literally hoist itself to the top of the incline. The winch would then be "fouled" or fastened down at the top of the grade and used to raise and lower log cars and even small locomotives up and down the incline.

One of the most daring engineering feats in logging railroad history was built by W.B. Townsend's Little River Lumber Company

**Montvale's Climax Loco on Eagle Creek .**

COURTESY OF GSMNP

**Swinging railroad bridge, Little River Railroad.**

on the Tennessee side of the Smokies. A swinging bridge incline (with crossties and tracks attached to steel cables) that was suspended above the East Fork of the Little River at the mouth of Meigs Creek must have brought chills to everyone involved each time a car was hoisted across.

Logging historians agree that the most unique transportation set-up in the southern Appalachians was achieved by Kitchens Lumber Company. James, John, and Charles Kitchens had established their lumber company in Ashland, Kentucky and had first logged in the Smokies while clearing the reservoir for the Aluminum Company of America's (Alcoa) Cheoah Dam and Lake. The brothers had acquired approximately 20,000 acres in the Twenty Mile Creek watershed and commenced a logging operation there in 1921. After 1919, when Cheoah Lake was completed, the only access to Twenty Mile Creek was by foot trail or boat. They built their town, Kitchensville, and eight-foot band-type sawmill at the east end of the new lake near where the rock quarry below

Fontana Dam is today.

A four mile standard gauge railroad was constructed from Kitchensville to Montvale's town of Fontana and the terminus of the Carolina & Tennessee Southern Railroad. To connect the sawmill and the timber reserve on Twenty Mile Creek, the brothers, who had prior maritime experience, constructed a 50-foot long stern-paddlewheel steamboat christened the *Vivian* after Charlie's wife. Designed for heavy tug boat type work, the craft was built of the finest white oak lumber and powered by an upright boiler steam engine that had been used by Southern Railway to power steam drills. A number of large barges were built to haul logs and materials. A steam powered log loader that resembled a small crane was manufactured by the American Hoist and Derrick Company of St. Paul, Minnesota. This was mounted on a floating platform to complete Kitchen's navy.

Next, two Hiesler geared locomotives, log cars, flat cars, rail-

**Kitchen's Navy at the mouth of Twenty Mile Creek on Cheoah Lake. The Vivian and barges are at lower right, floating American log loader in center, and log train at left.**

HOLLAND COLLECTION

road rails and ties, hardware, building materials to construct bunkhouses, cookhouses, shops, and everything else needed for a large logging operation were loaded onto the barges and steamed down to the mouth of Twenty Mile Creek. Approximately 16 miles of narrow gauge railway was built up Twenty Mile Creek and its tributaries to carry the logs down to the lake where they were loaded on barges with the American loader and then pushed up the lake to the sawmill with the *Vivian*.

A number of tales have survived the years concerning the *Vivian's* steamwhistle. Joseph P. Sluder, whose mother Julie ran a logging camp boardinghouse on Twenty Mile Creek, recounted to Tennessee journalist Vic Weals that Luther Anthony, Captain of the *Vivian*, "learned to play its steam whistle to imitate the call of the whippoorwill, that was a beautiful sound—more beautiful every time we heard it." Alberta and Carson Brewer reported in their book *Valley So Wild* that "a sawmill engine powered it, and its whistle could not be ignored. The *Vivian* drew several large barges, piled high with lumber up the river to the waiting locomotive, *Big Junaluska*. When the cargo was transferred both boat and train let out ear-splitting whistles to seal the transaction and set mountains trembling for miles." My favorite steam whistle story is a little holiday tale I wrote years ago for a Thanksgiving celebration at Fontana Village. While composing the piece, I relied on the old mountain story tellers axiom—"Tis a poor piece of cloth that can stand no embroidery."

### Turkeys and Steamwhistles

Fall had come on fast in the Smoky Mountains. The trees were bare and the acorns had fallen. This fall of 1921 produced an outstanding mast crop. Mast is the collective name given to acorns and seed pods of all the myriad trees found in this botanical storehouse and comprises a primary food source for the black bears and wild hogs that call these woods home.

But it was turkeys, not bears and boars that for two weeks now had dominated the thoughts of the old mountain veteran Will Orr. Old man Will and his family homesteaded on a mountain side plot located on the north shore of Cheoah Lake. He was known far and wide for his ability as a hunter and marksman. But this season had been different; Will suspected that all the commotion caused by the Kitchens Lumber Co. starting up operations on nearby Twenty Mile Creek was to blame for his poor success at bagging that Thanksgiving bird.

Kitchens operations were unique in that the logs were brought down Twenty Mile by narrow gauge Hiesler locomotives then loaded on barges by a floating American loader then steamed up the lake to the sawmill with the Vivian, named after company president Charles Kitchens wife. Each time the little steamboat and its raft of log laden barges passed by old man Will's place, the captain sounded his steam whistle, Will became less and less enamored by this constant reminder of the "progress" that had reached his remote corner of the back of beyond.

Finally, the day before Thanksgiving, Will located fresh sign aways up from his house and not far from the lake. He stalked the fine gobbler for about an hour to get the best shot. Finally the stage was set and the players in place, just as Will raised his faithful rifle the mountains reverberated with the scream of that god awful steam whistle—exit turkey.

Will had all he could stand, he went straight away to the sawmill and told that boat captain in no uncertain terms not to blow that dad burn whistle around his place any more. The loggers began to kid the old man that it was not the whistle but his poor aim that caused the absence of bird on his Thanksgiving table. This did not set too well with the old man and he headed back home. That evening as the Vivian headed back down the lake past Will's place the cocky captain laid down on his steam whistle. Then, with one shot, at 150 yards, the old man and his trusty rifle removed the whistle from the top of the stack on the bobbing steamboat. This, of course, released all the steam and set the boat adrift. Early the next morning after the loggers had secured their floundering boat and made temporary repairs, Mr. Charles Kitchens paid a visit to Will Orr. Charles Kitchens had learned over his years of back country logging that an irate mountain man is not conducive to good business management. Mr. Kitchens presented Mr. Orr with one of the fine store bought turkeys he had imported for his logging camps and apologized that the repast might not be as tasty as the wild version but hoped he would accept the token of friendship. Mr. Orr graciously accepted. By the way, the boat captain never blew his whistle in front of old man Will Orr's place again, and the loggers never again kidded the old man about his skill with a rifle. Old man Will really did shoot the whistle off the steamboat; I made up the part about the turkey.

While Norwood and Whiting set up operations at existing settlements with at least limited services, Ritter, Montvale, and

**Montvale Coronet Band, 1912.**

Kitchens had to start from scratch and construct complete towns and manufacturing facilities to support their operations. Obviously each lumber town was different, but they all contained certain obligatory components such as employee housing, a train station, a commissary or company store, and at least one community building that could double as school and church. The lumber companies in the Fontana area built towns that were quite elaborate. They believed that happy and contented workers were productive workers and provided entertainment, recreational, and social activities.

Montvale organized the Montvale Coronet Band. Ritter published a monthly company newspaper with tidbits from their operations around the country and in Europe entitled *The Hardwood Bark*. Some of the entries from Hazel Creek demonstrated a competitive spirit between the different divisions: "It seems that 16,786 feet is going to be the 1922 record for planing mill production in ten hours, for we have been running beech, birch and maple this month, and in spite of all our efforts, we have not been able to beat our oak run of August 4; however, we have made an average daily run of slightly over 14,000 feet, and unless we hear of anything to the contrary from some other source, we will lay claim to this additional record; and as the year is so nearly spent, we feel confident that you will concede to us the further honor of maintaining our own trumpeter." Some were gossipy: "The Athletic Branch of our Community Club, under the direction of Mr. Arthur

Danielson, has the makin's of a pretty good ball team, from which we expect to derive many entertaining games this season; and as our tennis court is being shaved, trimmed, manicured and garbed in the latest fashions of nets and racquets, those who favor this pastime will have no cause to complain of lack of facilities to indulge in it. The Entertainment Branch of our Club is providing Picture Shows followed by a dance, every Saturday night, and the Educational Branch, under the guidance of the Rev. J.H. Wilson, has organized a Literary Club, of which Mr. J. Berger is President; Mr. N.D. Moore, Vice-President; Mr. A.J. Rickman, Secretary, and Rev. J.H. Wilson, Critic." And some were comical: "Mrs. Charley Wilson, on seeing Arthur Watkins getting wood the other day, ran over to see if Mrs. Watkins was sick."

A wonderful description of the town of Proctor and life therein is given by historian and former resident Duane Oliver in his book *Hazel Creek Then and Now*. This description can't be improved upon and is therby reprinted here with the author's permission:

> Proctor, as planned and built by Ritter, was a complete town that was home to over a thousand people. It included, when finished, a school, a large commissary that housed the post office, company of-

**Judson, North Carolina.**

OLIVER COLLECTION

**Hazel Creek home, notice man on roof.**

fices and a considerable number of store rooms; there was also a barber shop, a large depot and a number of large houses on one side of the creek. On the other side were a cafe, a large two-story Baptist church, several rows of smaller houses, and a community building that held a pool hall barber shop and movie theatre. On the mountainside above the mill and pond were a large club house, a boarding house and several large houses, and continuing on around the mountain up the valley was a subdivision of houses known as North Proctor. Most houses on the commissary side and club house hill were large and comfortable with from six to nine rooms, and were constructed for company officials such as foremen. Those on the opposite side of the creek were smaller and built for regular employees of the company.

Because of the types of houses and their inhabitants, the street or road containing the larger homes and commissary was called Struttin' Street, a name given in gentle irony by the local people. The opposite side, with its smaller houses, was called Calico Street. Club House Hill was the name evolved for the section containing the club house and largest houses. When it was all finished, Proctor was a company town in every sense of the word except that the buildings were not small and cheaply constructed as was common in most cotton mill and mining towns.

The houses and commercial buildings were not original in style or design but were what is usually referred to as carpenter's design-book architecture which was being built all over America at the time. They were simple and solid, four-square structures not in any of the then-fashionable period styles such as Gothic, Queen Anne or Georgian. To have built in these styles would have taken longer and been more expensive to construct due to extra turned and scroll-saw woodwork required by them. And they would have been, in no way, any better structures. The buildings were as permanent as any wooden buildings of the period ever were and, in addition, Ritter planned to move to another location, which he did, when Hazel Creek was logged over.

The absence of decorative woodwork is not meant to imply that the buildings of Proctor were cheaply or thinly constructed. Since Ritter produced an immense amount of the finest quality lumber, the company never stinted in its use and built fine buildings of which everyone was proud and which, thirty years later, were still structurally sound. The carpenters used the then comparatively new "balloon" construction, which is how wooden houses are still built. The proliferation of sawmills in the 19th century as well as the seemingly inexhaustible amount of timber easily available changed wooden buildings from the previous log and heavy timber construction to that of building a frame of comparatively heavy members and facing the exterior and interior with layers of thinly sawn lumber, leaving a hollow space in the walls which is today filled with insulation.

All of this was made possible by the standardization, about the middle of the 19th century, of lumber into what we have today: 2 by 4's, 1 by 6's, etc., matched and standardized tongue-and-groove flooring and wall and ceiling covering, and machine production of nails of standardized sizes. In addition, machine-made and printed wallpaper as well as factory-produced paint and heavy tar-paper roofing were all easily available due to the industrial revolution of the 19th century. Ritter, of course, could produce all of his own lumber, and, by buying in large quantities, inexpensively obtain glass, paint, roofing, wiring, nails, phone and electrical cable, bricks and bathroom and kitchen plumbing fixtures.

If we buy a 2 by 4 today it is planed smooth and is less than two by four inches. In the period when Ritter was building Proctor, all framing lumber such as these were rough-sawn and the full size. Rough-sawn planks, such as used for subflooring and roofing, were a full inch thick. Timber used for floor joists was often three inches thick and twelve to fourteen inches wide. This extra thickness and width guaranteed solid houses whose floors did not sag.

Ritter covered the exterior of his buildings with planed, horizontally attached siding; interiors were finished in what was called ceiling. This name derived from the tightly put together covering inside a ship that aided in sealing in or in making it water-tight. In addition, this lumber was often used in the period to make room and porch ceilings and was originally developed for that purpose. This ceiling material was thin (¼ inch), planed, tongue-and-groove wood between three and four inches wide, with a bead groove down the center of each strip. It was attached horizontally to the wall and ceiling framing with the same technique with which tongue-and-groove oak flooring was laid over the inch-thick rough-sawn subflooring in all of the Ritter buildings at Proctor.

All of the buildings had running water, it being piped in from large, concrete reservoirs built where needed. These and a few foundation stones and bricks are about all that remain physically of Proctor today. The houses did not have septic tanks but drained through clay sewer pipes into the creek. At first, the houses did not have interior bathrooms, all of those on the creek in "downtown" Proctor having out-houses hanging over the creek in front of each house. To simplify construction of these buildings, some of them were built two to a platform with a common gangway running from the edge of the street. This arrangement was unsightly and unpleasant, so rather soon these structures were torn down and bathrooms built into each house or out-houses constructed in the rear.

The depot was painted grey and the other buildings were all painted white on the outside with, unfortunately, lead-based paint which was about all, except for whitewash, was manufactured at the time. This was unfortunate because Vate Payne, in painting these buildings, got blood poisoning and died from it. The interior of these buildings, with their twelve-foot high ceilings, were painted in pastel colors with either enamel or calcimine, which is a paint made with calcium carbonate, powdered glue and pigment. This whitewash-like paint was the predecessor of the water-based latex and acrylic wall paints of today. It came in a powdered from and the house painter just added water and stirred. Because of the glue in it, it did not flake off as does white-

The Back of Beyond Booms **95**

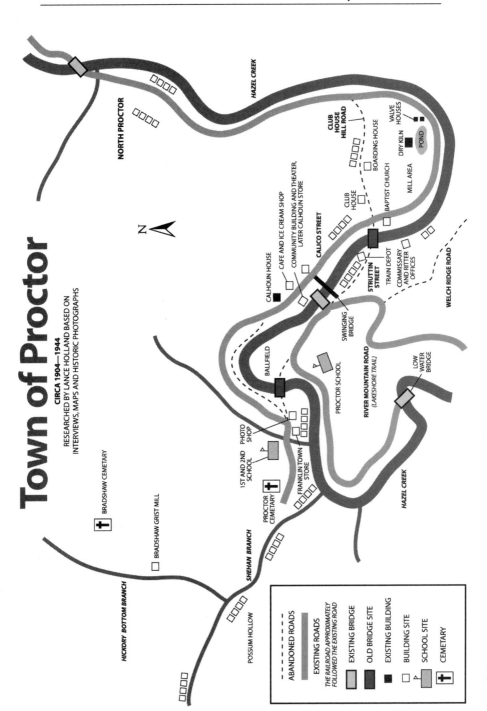

wash, from which it derived. Unlike some of today's paints, it had a pleasant odor and was very inexpensive, being adopted by the regular inhabitants of the creek when they wished to paint the interior of their houses.

A white picket fence ran down the streets in front of the houses, and a row of sugar maples was planted on both sides of the streets. Since Proctor's streets were not paved or even gravelled, a boardwalk was built down both Struttin' and Calico Streets in front of the houses. Those living on Club House Hill also had a boardwalk which turned into a long set of steps starting near the church. When it was all finished, with its white buildings, maple trees, picket fences and boardwalks, Proctor presented a most pleasing appearance.

Before Ritter built the town of Proctor, the post office was in J.W. Bradshaw's store which was near where the mill pond was made. This is the same Bradshaw who was taken to court in 1907 by the Smoky Mountain Railway Company to condemn an eighty-foot wide strip of his and J.W. Welch's land running from the school's ball field up the creek. Since the railway went up the Struttin' Street's side of the creek and followed the curve of the creek to the right in front of the commissary and two or so more houses, at which point it crossed the creek to continue on up, as the court order states, to Bone Valley, Bradshaw and Welch originally owned that side of Proctor. Bradshaw certainly owned part, and probably all, of the large field where the pond, mill and lumber yard were to be located, and Welch had originally owned what became known as North Proctor where he had built a house but did not like the location due to the noise of the creek.

Bradshaw knew that once the commissary was built his store would cease to have any customers. Perhaps this, in addition to not wanting to part with his fine land and feeling that he was not offered enough, which he probably wasn't, was the most basic reason he did not want to sell to the railroad. In the end, he sold all of his land at Proctor to Ritter and moved away.

Whatever Bradshaw's problems, we must sympathize with this pioneer, and the post office was placed in the commissary when it was constructed. The white-painted commissary was a large structure with a tall, false front as was fashionable for stores at the time, and with a wide, unroofed porch running its length. Also opening off the porch was a company office, and in the back and to the sides were storerooms and a suite of rooms with a covered porch that was later used as an apartment after Ritter left the area.

The high-ceilinged, oak-floored interior of the commissary was arranged like an old-fashioned country store, which it was, except that it was not old-fashioned then. A wide counter ran around three sides of the large room with shelves up to the ceiling behind this. The commissary did not have a freezer or refrigerator, but ice was brought in on the train so that drinks could be kept cold in drink boxes. Local people could also buy ice for their ice boxes. The store carried pretty much what you would expect to find in a general store, and a great deal more of everything and an immensely wider variety than Bradshaw, Jones, Medlin or Coburn had sold in their little stores since the 1880's. The commissary did not carry fresh vegetables or meat, but most people had a garden, and vegetables and meat, especially chickens, could be bought from local people along with eggs, butter and berries. Fresh beef, however, was available for awhile from someone who opened a slaughterhouse on the edge of the school's ballfield. It was closed after awhile since it did not meet sanitary conditions and had no refrigeration. After Ritter left in 1928, the field where it was located grew up in broomsedge and the area was littered with sun-bleached bones for decades.

The commissary did not have a scrip system of exchange, which is certainly a point in Ritter's favor; charge accounts, however could be arranged at the stores.

The other place where food could be bought in Proctor was at a little cafe near the community building or theatre on Calico Street. This was run by Martin and Rachel Hyde and sold soft drinks, candy, tobacco and, most popular, ice cream. This was the first sold on Hazel Creek and the first that the majority of the local people had seen. It, like everything else there, was brought in on the train, arriving in large containers on ice, and sold out quickly. People who did not buy it in cones brought with them a small pail to be filled at the cafe and then hurried home.

A small barber shop was built at the end of the train depot, beside the bridge and across the creek from the church which was at the end of Calico Street.

Before the Ritter era, the only church in Proctor was a small school/church building of rough lumber out in Possum Hollow or Franklin Town as it came to be called. There were also small churches in Bone Valley and on Cable Branch. The church that Ritter built at Proctor was good-sized, and was ceiled inside with a high, flat ceiling. There was a second floor with a large room and several smaller ones for storage and lodge meetings. With the arrival of numerous new people to work for Ritter, the church's activities were expanded to include a Sunday School and other activities, and ministers who preached on a regular basis were drawn to it.

At the other, or lower, end of Calico Street was the community building or movie theatre, a large two-story structure covered in rough-sawn boards and unpainted on the outside. This building was to the immediate left at the end of the bridge that one crosses today to get to the Bradshaw and Proctor Cemeteries or Calhoun house. The top floor contained a pool hall and a barber shop and was reached by an outside staircase. Short, or bobbed, hair for women came into fashion in the 1920's, and most of the girls had their hair cut here by John Hicks, the barber at this shop.

The movie theatre, which seated two or three hundred, was on the ground floor and like ice cream, was a novelty and delight for the majority of the residents, especially the younger people. Not everyone, however, approved of movies, especially the Reverend Stansberry who was the pastor of the church at the time. Seating was on benches and the movie screen was at the back of a small stage down front. This was the time of silent movies. As the dialogue flashed on the screen the audience read it out loud. Not all of the audience could read, however, so the "sound" provided by the readers was a convenience for them. A player piano sat down front, and this was frantically pumped to provide music. Granville Calhoun, who managed the theatre from 1913 to 1918, hired a Negro family band from Franklin to provide music, especially when the film broke. Movies showed on Wednesday and Saturday nights, and were mainly westerns, Charlie Chaplin and Fatty Arbuckle. Admission was ten cents. There was no concession stand in the theatre but patrons could get something to eat and drink at the nearby cafe. The new school did not as yet have an auditorium and once, about 1922, Zina Farley Oliver played Ichabod Crane in a play presented in the theatre, and for makeup blackened her face with shoe polish or "shoe black". It is painful to think of how much scrubbing this later took to remove. There was a suspension or swinging bridge across the creek at the theatre, a little above where the present bridge is located. People from some distance away coming to the movies had to carry an oil lantern which they usually left at the end of the bridge and then retrieved and lighted for their trip home.

Up on the hill above the pond and mill was a row of large houses, a club house and a boarding house. The boarding house did not serve meals, and those staying there took their meals at the club house. Mel

Rogers, who was an excellent cook, was the cook here. Staying at the boarding house were some of the regular employees of the lumber company, teachers, and people who had non-lumber jobs such as workers on the new county road being built from Bryson City to Proctor and Fontana.

The club house, the most imposing building in Proctor, was a large, three-story structure with verandahs on the first two floors across the front of it. The ground floor contained, at the back, a large kitchen and pantry, with the front composed of two large dining rooms in which people staying here and at the boarding house took their meals.

The second floor, which could be reached by stairs from the dining area or by a flight of steps on the exterior at the end of the porch, contained the cook's quarters as well as a lounge and bedrooms for guests and important employees of the company such as the company doctor and dentist. The third floor, reached from the hallway of the second floor, contained large bedrooms for special company guests.

When Ritter cut its last tree and moved out of Hazel Creek in 1928, this building was no longer needed as a club house and was rented to private individuals as a residence. My Aunt Rachel and Uncle Martin Hyde, who was the last postmaster at Proctor, lived here for several years when I was a child. I always greatly enjoyed visiting them for the house was wonderfully large. Some of the original furnishings remained and they were what you would have found in a gentleman's club of the period, which it was. I recall heavy, dark oak furniture in the then-popular Mission Style, a horse-hair sofa and chairs that tickled my bare legs, a badly out-of-tune piano that no one could play, claw-foot cast-iron bath tubs, dark, shiny oak floors and woodwork, on the walls steel engravings of mythological scenes, paintings on glass, sepia-tone copper engravings, and in the dining room colored prints of dead rabbits and fish guaranteed to destroy any but the strongest appetites but which were very fashionable for dining rooms at the turn of the century.

The Hydes lived on the second and third floors, so I have no idea of what treasures, if any, the first floor contained. Aunt Rachel always said it was damp and dark, which I am sure it was for it was built almost directly on the ground as were most houses of the time. The third floor, mainly large, empty rooms, had one unused room that contained dozens and dozens of empty thread spools. During World War I some of the Ritter ladies had done some sort of sewing in this room for the soldiers. They had left all of those wonderful empty spools that had lain there undisturbed for almost twenty years until I discovered them.

The club house was built against the mountainside and behind the kitchen was a large, long room that must have originally been a combination pantry and storeroom. The floor was about to fall through in places, the room was full of discarded furniture, and on the walls hung moth-eaten animal heads. Perhaps some of these had been shot by gentlemen staying at the club. The room was dark, musty and damp, and to a child, deliciously scary.

To finish with the club house, on the wall of the second floor entrance hall was a large, long-defunct turn-of-the-century wall phone in an oak case. What delighted me most, however, was an ornate brass doorbell mounted in the center of the heavy front door just below the beveled glass panes. It could be rung like an old-fashioned bicycle bell, by twisting a little handle, and I could not resist ringing it every time I used the door.

Continuing on around the club house road, or going up the road past the mill, was North Proctor. Most of this was the "colored town", and its houses were built with the same care and quality as was the rest of Proctor. The small community of blacks worked for Ritter in the same type jobs as did the whites, and they were the first blacks to live on the creek. There was, however, no integration of church or school. They did not have their own church building but had services in each other's houses. The local people enjoyed going up to North Proctor and singing with the black population.

The village of Ritter, built at the river at the creek's mouth at the juncture of the Smoky Mountain and Southern Railways, was not really a town but was a settlement composed of a few houses and a depot.

With such a large-scale venture employing several hundred people in dangerous jobs, Ritter had to have a resident company doctor. For this purpose Ritter brought in Dr. J.G. Storie from West Virginia where Ritter also had a timber operation. He lived in the clubhouse and had an office down in Proctor. Not only did he tend to the various illnesses and accidents of company employees but his services were available to everyone in the area regardless of whether they or their family were Ritter employees. He was the first and last resident doctor on the creek.

One of his duties was, on a set schedule, to go up the railroad as far as it went and tend to those at the logging camps and along the way who needed his care. To do this, he rode up on the train in the morning but coasted back down to Proctor on a little railway car called a "speeder" that was constructed just for his use. It was small and light, being made of tubing like a four-wheeled bicycle. It had a seat, pedals, brake and a basket in which he carried his little black bag and extra medical supplies. There was no pharmacy to which people could go to have a prescription filled, so he had to take with him all the medicine that he knew from experience he might need. Everyone knew on what days, and the approximate time he pedaled down the creek so that anyone who needed medical attention could flag him down. He would brake to a halt, and if necessary remove the speeder from the tracks if he had help, and tend to the patient. When the house call was over and the speeder back on the tracks, he would continue coasting or pedaling back down the creek to Proctor. There was also a company dentist who, like Dr. Storie, provided service to everyone from his office in Proctor.

Not structurally part of Proctor's buildings but nonetheless important was the fact that the town had phones and electric lights. Phones ran to all of the important houses, clubhouse, commissary, theatre, offices, sawmill and up the creek so that everyone who needed to could stay in touch. This was the first and last phone system in Proctor. Electricity was provided at the sawmill by a steam generator, and power was run to all of the company buildings, houses and sawmill, which was electrically powered.

When Ritter arrived in 1903 and decided to log Hazel Creek, the company realized that the existing one-room school on Shehan Branch would be much too small for the expected increase in population. As discussed earlier, the lower section of the creek had built a one-room log church and school house in the 1870's on land donated by J.W. Welch. Later, when Ritter arrived and began the construction of the town of Proctor and sawn lumber was easily available about 1909 or so a second one-room church and school was built just below the original log one. This was used only a short time until Ritter completed the con-

**Preacher Ottie Vance returning from Bone Valley Church on his "speeder".**

**Proctor School.**

struction of a church and a new Proctor school about 1914 or a little earlier.

The new school had rooms for four teachers and was also on land donated by J.W. Welch. There is now a horse-tethering area where the Proctor school once stood, and the school's playground and ballfield, through which the railroad once ran, is now the Proctor campground. This new school was built with white-painted siding and ceiled interiors, and with a bell-tower whose bell is in the possession of Mrs. E.H. Oliver.

This school was consolidated in 1934 and renamed the Calhoun-Coburn School. At this time an auditorium and additional classrooms were added as it became a high school. Some of the Ritter era teachers at this school were Mary Hall, Joe Wilson, Pearly Brendle, Mary Wilson, Grace Wilson, Polly Stuart, Lottie Debord, Rowe Henry, Wilie Rhea, Maude Wiggins, R. Hyatt, Ms. West and Elvira Welch. For a short time Elvira lived in one of the company's little rail houses that was set up near the school's ballfield. She had had polio as a child and since her family's home was on Welch Ridge, a considerable distance away, it was more convenient for her to live in close proximity to the school. In 1917-1918 R.L. Randolph was the Principal and I.G. Horner was his assistant at this school. During the Ritter era Miss Emma Galloway taught at Medlin and Miss Louada Burnett taught at Cable Branch. There were also schools *at Camp Seven, Walkers Creek, Proctor Creek and Sugar Fork.*

*So far, I have dealt primarily with the Ritter enterprise and era from the standpoint of the logging-lumber aspect and the building of the railroad and town of Proctor. As is obvious, about 1900 a distinct change had begun to take place not only on Hazel Creek but throughout the entire Smokies. The force most directly responsible for this change was mechanized logging such as that done by Ritter and the numerous other logging companies that discovered the southern Appalachians around the turn of the century. The economy, almost overnight, changed from one of self-sufficiency, subsistence and barter to one where there was a considerable amount of 'real' money.*

Even though Proctor has been called the finest of the Smoky Mountain lumber towns, the other lumber towns in the Fontana area had similar facilities and lifestyles. Of course, the reason for the towns was the production of lumber. Each company constructed a large mechanized sawmill. The sawmills used huge band saws rather than circular saws to rough saw the timber. Sev-

**Almond School.**

HOLLAND COLLECTION

**Ritter Lumber Company's Hazel Creek Operation.**

eral of the companies had dry kilns and planing mills. Some even had dimension mills and flooring factories. In the case of Ritter Lumber Company, the virgin timber of Hazel Creek was processed into the finest strip and parquet flooring and shipped via their offices in Liverpool, London, Glasgow, Antwerp, and Cologne, ultimately gracing the floors of some of Europe's grandest buildings. As one can see, these were not small time, backwoods sawmillers, they were some of the most advanced industrialists in the world. In fact, *The Hardwood Bark* reported in September 1922 that the W.M. Ritter Company "Has 11 band mills, 11 planing mills, 11 flooring units, 8 dimension mills, 6 dry kilns, comprising 20 batteries, 14 logging operations, operates 187 miles of railroad, and its plants in the aggregate cover 96 $1/2$ acres of floor space and its loading docks and piling spaces cover 407 acres of land. Its properties are scattered over five states and extend into nine counties. Its manufacturing capacity is 125,000,000 board feet annually. It is the largest producer of hardwood in the world."

By the late 1920's all of the reasonably accessible and available timber had been harvested from the region. One by one, the lumber companies disassembled their mills and plants, sold off their

COURTESY OF GSMNP

real estate holdings, and even took up their railroad tracks as they left the area. The idea of sustainable forestry was just in its infancy; ironically, also in western North Carolina, on George Vanderbilt's Biltmore Estate.

Many local inhabitants were now second generation timbermen and went with the logging companies to their next locations. Strong ties to the southern Appalachians are still held by many loggers in the Pacific Northwest. A number of people imported by the lumber companies liked the area and stayed after the departure of the companies. A notable example was Ritter's chief civil engineer, Orson P. Burlingame, who came to Hazel Creek in 1902, married a local girl, Lillie Lucille Brooks, and built a fine 14 room home on Hazel Creek. After Ritter left the area, Burlingame served as the Swain County civil engineer. He is buried in the Bone Valley Cemetery.

The 25 or so years that the big lumber companies held sway in the Fontana area took many of the inhabitants from a pioneer/subsistence lifestyle to the forefront of American technology. The land itself was certainly left with thousands of acres of cutover stubble, but also all the homes, businesses, roads, and bridges that were built during the logging years had rendered the Fontana area in 1930 a much different place than it was in 1900. A poem

**Sanders Calhoun's store, Wayside.**

published in the January 1925 edition of the *Hardwood Bark* sums up the change:

**Reversed**
Twenty years ago today a wilderness was here;
A man with powder in his gun went forth to hunt a deer;
But now the times have changed somewhat—are on a different plan,
A dear, with powder on her nose, goes forth to hunt a man.

The Back of Beyond Booms **107**

*Ritter's Sawmill and log pond (above), and lumber yard (below).*

*Chapter 8*

# Better Late Than Never

The idea of preserving a vast area of forestland in the eastern United States was first publicly proposed in the 1880's by Reverend C.D. Smith of Franklin, North Carolina and Dr. Henry O. Marcy of Boston, Massachusetts. They heralded the region as an outstanding health resort. In 1891, while visiting George Vanderbilt at the Biltmore Estate, Joseph A. Holmes, the North Carolina state geologist, suggested to Gifford Pinchot, the first American trained in Germany in the new science of forestry and then forester for the Biltmore Estate, that a great national forest for the southern Appalachians be established. Pinchot would later become the first chief of the newly formed U.S. Forest Service. A committee formed by the Asheville Board of Trade, including Dr. Chase P. Ambler and George Vanderbilt, arranged a gathering at Asheville on November 11, 1899, of 42 statesmen, industrialists, newspapermen and other influential people that organized the Appalachian National Park Association. A "memorial" of this association was presented to Congress on January 2, 1901. Later that year, Congress appropriated $5,000 for the Secretary of Agriculture through the Division of Forestry and the U.S. Geological Survey to study the southern Appalachian forests. An area of 9,600,000 acres were examined and mapped. Gifford Pinchot later wrote of this study:

> *The results were set forth in an elaborate report transmitted to Congress with a message on December 19, 1901, by Theodore Roosevelt,*

and ordered printed as Senate Document N. 84. That document contained reliable information concerning the proposed Appalachian Forest Reserve, and gave exhaustive data on the composition, condition, character, extent, and distribution of the forests of a region then little known.

This is the same public document referred to earlier in Chapter 5, commonly referred to as the Roosevelt Report.

The situation in the east was much different than in the western United States, where national parks had been carved from existing government land, starting with Yellowstone in 1872 and followed by Sequoia, General Grant (later Kings Canyon), and Yosemite in 1890. In 1900 almost all of the land east of the Mississippi was under private ownership and the government had no program to purchase land for forest preservation. During the next decade, repeated legislation was submitted to Congress to fund an eastern forest reserve with very little success. Resistance such as that of republican Joseph G. Cannon, Speaker of the House, whose position was "not one cent for scenery" was hard to overcome. Finally in March of 1911, the Weeks Act became law and enabled the federal government to purchase "forested, cutover, or denuded lands on the headwaters of and vital to the flow of navigable streams." The Clarke-McNary Amendment in 1924 enabled the purchase of any desirable forest lands.

The nine year period between the Roosevelt Report and Recommendation in 1902 and the passage of the Weeks Act in 1911 had given the Forest Service ample time to decide what areas would be recommended for the establishment of national forests in the eastern United States at the onset of the program. Seven purchase units in the southern region, including the Nantahala, were recommended and approved on March 27, 1911, by the National Forest Reservation Commission. The first actual purchase of forest land in western North Carolina was made on August 29, 1911, of 8,100 acres in McDowell County from Burke McDowell Lumber Company for $7.00 per acre.

A certain amount of land had to actually be acquired before a purchase unit could officially become a national forest. The Nantahala region was first proclaimed a national forest by President Woodrow Wilson on January 20, 1920, with a gross area of 812,134 acres. This proclamation, however, did not include "the portion of Swain County lying west of the Nantahala River and the portion of Cherokee County lying north and east of Murphy, North Carolina and all of Graham County," roughly today's Cheoah Ranger District. Then on March 25, 1921, a proclamation by President Warren G. Harding added the above portions of Cherokee, Graham, and Swain counties to the Pisgah National Forest. Finally, a proclamation dated October 10, 1929, by President Herbert Hoover restored to the Nantahala, the areas previously transferred to the Pisgah, expanding the Nantahala boundaries.

An examination of land purchase records at the U.S. Forest Service supervisors office in Asheville, North Carolina revealed that no land in the Fontana area was actually acquired by the Forest Service until after the construction of Fontana Dam when lands of the reservoir acquired by TVA were transferred to the Forest Service. Simultaneously, large tracts were purchased from Whiting Lumber Company, the J.E. Coburn estate, and others, resulting in about 95% of the south shore of Fontana Lake and surrounding area under the control of the U.S.F.S.

**The gentlemen's pastime of fly fishing.**

Much discussion and posturing occurred between 1900 and 1925 about whether any of the southern Appalachian forest should be preserved as a national park or managed as national forest. And if a park were to be created, where would it be? The lumbermen who owned vast tracts of the land always thought national forests were the best idea. Each region touted theirs as being perfect for the new park: Virginia had Shenandoah, Kentucky said Mammoth Cave was best. The North Carolina promoters had a plethora of choices; Linville–Grandfather Mountain, the Craggies, Mt. Mitchell, and the Smokies, while the Tennessee contingent praised the Smokies.

Early in 1924, Secretary of the Interior Hubert Work made known his desire to establish a park in the east and appointed the Southern Appalachian National Park Commission to study the entire mountain region. In July 1924 the five man committee began an inspection tour in Gainesville, Georgia. The group was met by part of the Asheville contingent at Highlands, North Carolina who made sure the committeemen were treated to the best western North Carolina had to offer. Soon after the entourage reached the Grove Park Inn in Asheville, a delegation from Knoxville arrived to try to persuade the committee to forgo investigating other sites in Carolina and come directly to the Tennessee side of the Smokies. This was the first overt, almost hostile, action in a competition between tourism and conservation promoters from the two states that continues today. Even the books written about the founding of the park often display bias depending on whether the author was a Tennessean or Carolinian.

*Horace Kephart, who lived in this cabin on the Little Fork of the Sugar Fork of Hazel Creek in the early 1900's, became one of the parents of the Great Smoky Mountains National Park.*

The Tennessee contingent organized the Great Smoky Mountains Conservation Association on December 21, 1923, electing Mr. Willis P. Davis, manager of the Knoxville Iron Company, as chairman. While vacationing in Yellowstone the previous summer, Mrs. Davis asked her husband "Why can't we have a national park in the Great Smokies?" Evidently, Mr. Davis thought it was a pretty good idea. Mrs. Davis has since been listed as the "mother" of the Great Smokies park. Another conservation association member, Colonel David C. Chapman, a wholesale druggist, became the workhorse of the park movement on the Tennessee side and is often referred to as the "father of the park." On the Carolina side, Horace Kephart, Mark Squires, and Dr. Ambler have all been referred to as the park's papa. Michael Frome in his book *Strangers In High Places* observes that "Pride of parenthood is well distributed after a beautiful baby is born."

Meanwhile, back at the Grove Park Inn, the Knoxville group went home empty-handed as the committee continued their planned itinerary. By the time the committee finally arrived in Knoxville, only the two most hardy members were up for more inspection. Travel through the southern Appalachians was quite laborious. The two remaining committeemen, Harlan P. Kelsey of Massachusetts and William C. Gregg of New York, were escorted by a large contingent of Tennesseans led by Colonel Chapman through the back country of the Smokies for almost a week.

Paul J. Adams, who would establish and manage the first permanent camp atop Mt. LeConte, which later became LeConte Lodge, was among the group and recounts part of the journey in his booklet *Mt. LeConte*. After leaving Cherokee Orchard outside Gatlinburg, only the first mile could be negotiated on horseback so the rest of the trip up and down Mt. LeConte was made on foot:

> Back then, one needed both strong legs and arms to gain the top of Rainbow Falls. The 'trail' went up a leaning tree near the bluff about 100 feet west of the falls. Helpers at the base of the tree helped some of our less agile guests to reach the first tree branches. Others at the top helped them from the tree to solid ground. But everyone had to climb the middle distance under his own power.

Before daylight the next morning after camping near the summit of Mt. LeConte, the group headed for Myrtle Point. The Adams narrative continues:

> Rain fell during the night and the Colonel feared we would not be able to see a beautiful sunrise from Myrtle Point. But we started toward the Point anyway, at the first streak of dawn.
>
> We were a motley crew as we headed up across Clifftop, climbing single file toward Myrtle Point. Most of us had blankets around our shoulders to protect us from the rain-wet bushes. We had had coffee

but nothing else before leaving camp. Every third or fourth man carried a lantern and a few had flashlights. The lanterns were left beside the trail after we crossed Clifftop, because the sky had lightened enough for us to see without them.

The sky overhead was clear. But we looked down on billowing tops of thunderheads in the valleys. A south breeze touched us lightly. We knew stronger winds were at work below us. They were whipping and tumbling the thunderheads.

Through a moderate haze in the east, we could see Mt. Guyot. And then the sun, a ball of red fire, rose over Guyot. Its rays sparkled splendor in the cloudtops below us.

The winds in the clouds grew more restless, began to agitate them more violently. Great chunks of clouds began to rip loose from the main mass and rise a thousand feet. As they arose, they sometimes briefly blocked the sun. A constant wind picked up these cloud chunks and hustled them off to the northwest.

We were small spectators, awe-struck by the vast, primitive beauty of an extra-special Myrtle Point sunrise.

The group descended LeConte via Alum Cave Bluff on a trail that had been blazed and chopped out only a few days earlier. Steep rock faces to cross, a few minor injuries, and a rendezvous with horses that did not happen all contributed to a very arduous tour.

Despite the hardships, Mr. Kelsey and Mr. Gregg must have been thoroughly impressed. The Southern Appalachian National Park Commission met in December of 1924 and published their findings:

> We inspected the northern part of Georgia, whose fine mountains blend with the Highland region of southern North Carolina. We ascended Mount Mitchell and viewed the splendid Black Mountain Range north of Asheville. We went over carefully the Grandfather Mountain region, which for our study included the beautiful country from Blowing Rock to the remarkable Linville Gorge. We responded to the call of the poet—to see Roan Mountain if we would really see the southern Appalachians. We went to Knoxville and from there to the tops of the 'Big Smokies', which carry on their crest the boundary line between North Carolina and Tennessee. We went into Virginia to inspect that portion of the Blue Ridge on the east side of the Shenandoah Valley

which extends from Front Royal to Waynesboro. Some members of the committee also visited Cumberland Gap, southern West Virginia, northern Alabama, and eastern Kentucky. Several areas were found that contained topographic features of great scenic value, where waterfalls, cascades, cliffs, and mountain peaks, with beautiful valleys lying in their midst, gave ample assurance that any or all of these areas were possible for development into a national park which would compare favorably with any of the existing national parks in the West.

Charged with the responsibility of picking the best site, the committee reported:

The Great Smoky Mountains easily stand first because of the height of the mountains, depth of valleys, ruggedness of the area, and the unexampled variety of trees, shrubs and plants. The region includes Mount Guyot, Mount LeConte, Clingman's Dome, and Gregory Bald, and may be extended in several directions to include other splendid mountain regions adjacent thereto. The Blue Ridge of Virginia, one of the sections which had your committee's careful study, while secondary to the Great Smokies in altitude and some other features, constitutes in our judgment the outstanding and logical place for the creation of the first national park in the southern Appalachians. We hope it will be made into a national park and that its success will encourage the Congress to create a second park in the Great Smoky Mountains, which lie some 300 miles distant southwest.

Now that the federal government had made their decision, much work was to be done. First, all the regional promoters had to direct their energy toward a common goal. A booklet entitled *A National Park in the Great Smoky Mountains*, written by Horace Kephart and published by the Swain County Chamber of Commerce in 1925, stated that "For us Carolinians it is the Smoky Mountains or nothing." With Colonel Chapman leading the effort on the Tennessee side and state Senator Mark Squires of Lenoir as chairman of the North Carolina Park Commission, steady progress was made. Enabling legislation was passed and monies were appropriated by each legislature. A fund raising campaign was initiated in which even school children donated nickels and dimes to help buy park land. On March 30, 1928, John D. Rockefeller Jr., through the Laura Spelman Rockefeller Memorial, issued a grant of $5,000,000 to match funds donated by the governments, organizations, and people of the two states.

Congress repeatedly defeated bills to allocate money for the park, so President Franklin D. Roosevelt issued an executive order allocating $1,550,000 from funds authorized for the Civilian Conservation Corps and other purposes toward the purchase of park lands. Later Congress would appropriate funds to complete park purchases. By 1966, a combined total of $4,095,696 came about equally from the two states: $5,065,000 was donated by the Rockefeller Memorial; and $3,503,766 from the United States government was used to buy the land that is the Great Smoky Mountains National Park.

Arno B. Cammerer, then assistant director of the National Park Service took a very active role in the selection of the lands that would be purchased for the new park. Although a number of park boundaries had been proposed, Cammerer personally inspected the area and designated a proposed boundary, known as the Cammerer Line, that would be the actual boundary when the park was officially established on June 15, 1934. President Franklin Roosevelt would later dedicate the park in an elaborate ceremony at Newfound Gap on September 2, 1940.

***Early park road construction.***

Most of the early proposed boundaries had the Little Tennessee and Tuckasegee Rivers as the southern boundary of the park. The Cammerer Line excluded an irregular strip of about 46,000 acres north of the Little T. from Twenty Mile Creek east to a point near Bryson City—the Fontana area. One of the Southern National Park Commission's criteria for picking the new park location was that "It is also essential that the park sites should include no towns or industrial plants of magnitude, no valuable mineral holdings, no important water power sites, no railroads or other corporate interests with which difficulties of administration might arise." Even though many park promoters wanted the park to be contiguous

**Roosevelt at Park dedication.**

from the state line ridge down to the river, the fact that the Fontana area encompassed all of the above no-no's, coupled with limited funds probably resulted in Cammerer excluding the area from the original boundary. The northern half of the Fontana area would later be added to the Great Smoky Mountains National Park through an intriguing series of events.

Chapter 9

# River Becomes Resource

The morning that Attakullakulla stood on the edge of the bluff known as the Narrows, hearing the great river rush by below, he knew the river held great power. Indian people from time immemorial had revered the spiritual power in their myths and used the physical power to propel their canoes and fill the baskets of their fish traps. Many years later man would harness this power, but it was not the great government experiment, the Tennessee Valley Authority—with their corps of engineers and army of workers—that would precipitate the need to build huge hydroelectric dams deep in the mountain wilderness. It was an unemployed 22-year-old named Charles Martin Hall working in a woodshed in Oberlin, Ohio in 1886.

Copper was the metal that was extracted from the Fontana area in the greatest quantity. But aluminum was the metal that caused the greatest changes to occur to the land itself and to the people who lived there.

As early as 1807 an English electrochemist, Sir Humphry Davey, became convinced that the earth held a light weight, reasonably strong, and stable new metal he called aluminum. In 1825 H.C. Oersted, a Danish physicist and chemist actually produced a small lump of the shiny new metal. Other scientists refined the separation process but by 1880, at $8 per pound, aluminum had found few practical applications.

Charles Martin Hall, encouraged by his college chemistry pro-

*River scene—pre-dam (above). Charles Martin Hall (below).*

fessor, became absorbed with "thinking of a process for making aluminum cheaply." After a small accidental fire in his upstairs room, young Charles' experiments were moved out back to the family woodshed. Assisted by his sister Julia and using items such as mother's cookie jar as equipment, Hall tried to separate the metal by electrolysis. They prepared a mixture of bauxite, soda ash, lime, steam, and fuel oil to make unrefined alumina. The alumina was then combined with pitch, cryolite, and fluorspar and placed in a carbon lined vessel or "pot." On February 23, 1886, a considerable direct electric current was passed through the mixture for several hours. When the brew had cooled and solidified, it was broken open to reveal several shining buttons of aluminum.

Two years passed as Hall tried to get his process patented and find backers to try out the process on a commercial scale. In August of 1888, patent in hand, Hall linked up with Pittsburgh entrepreneurs Captain A.E. Hall and George H. Clapp, resulting in the formation of the Pittsburgh Reduction Company. This very successful early effort would in time become the Aluminum Company of America, shortened to Alcoa in 1907.

The two primary ingredients in the production of aluminum are bauxite and electricity. Bauxite was and still is relatively abundant and easily transported. Conversely, the electrical needs would become staggering. For example, during World War II when the American aluminum industry was producing over 2 billion pounds annually, T.D. Jolly, Alcoa's chief engineer, stated that "To produce 2,100,000,000 pounds of aluminum will require annually more electricity than was consumed in 1940 in 27 of the 48 states. In

**First aluminum plant of the Pittsburgh Reduction Company, later to become the Aluminum Company of America, ALCOA.**

ALCOA

one day the industry will draw more current than a city of 60,000 homes consumes in one year."

The growing need for electricity soon became apparent to the fledgling Pittsburgh Reduction Company, resulting in the construction of an aluminum plant at Niagara Falls, New York where cheap hydro power was available from the Niagara Falls Power Company. Charles C. Carr in Alcoa's corporate history states:

> *In placing an aluminum reduction works at Niagara Falls, the Company was inaugurating a policy Nature has imposed upon it, one of locating its aluminum reduction operations whenever possible near sources of hydroelectric energy. This custom has prevailed for a half century. It is easier to bring the raw materials to the vicinity of adequate hydro power than to send the electricity long distances to sections where raw materials are in abundance. In an advertisement in* The Saturday Evening Post *in 1937, Alcoa discussed this problem under a headline reading, 'Nature Located Things Badly for Making Aluminum in America'. Concerning the power problem, the Company said, 'It became*

**America's first pot line for making aluminum, production averaged fifty pounds per day.**

ALCOA

necessary to transport the unfinished product to distant places where great rivers run steep. In these locations, away from industrial centers, where there has been little demand for power, we must build great dams, reservoirs and powerhouses to make the essentially low-cost electricity which produces the virgin metal.

The company would develop hydro power at Shawinigin Falls in Canada and Massewa, New York on the St. Lawrence River, but still more power was needed. In 1909 Alcoa finally found its power bonanza, the Little Tennessee River. Mr. Carr reported:

*Spurred on by necessity, Mr. Davis and his associates started to acquire riparian properties along the Little Tennessee River and its tributaries in 1910. Studies and plans that contemplated the unified development of the entire river and its tributaries above Chilhowee, Tennessee, were undertaken. The assurance of adequate power from that swift-flowing mountain river and its tributaries, to be developed as needed, gave Mr. Davis the vision of what is today this country's largest aluminum plant, at Alcoa, Tennessee. On March 6, 1914, the first pot lines of an aluminum reduction works started operating at this location.*

Of course, the old nemesis of resource developers in the area—transportation—was the first problem to overcome. The only access from the aluminum plant site near Maryville, Tennessee to the new dam sites was the rough old wagon road completed in 1829 called the Parson's Turnpike. The first engineers and surveyors actually accessed the area on horseback via Bryson City and Robbinsville in North Carolina. The engineers picked a narrow gorge near the confluence of the Little T. and Cheoah Rivers for their first dam. They also chose the Hardin or Howard farm, later named Calderwood after construction superintendent I.G. Calderwood, ten miles downstream from the dam site where the river first leaves the high mountain gorge for their headquarters. The Howard farmhouse actually remained the general offices for all of Alcoa's Tennessee operations until 1957, when they were moved to the plant at Alcoa, Tennessee. Evidently the rail service to the new headquarters was not the best. Carson Brewer, in his book *Valley So Wild*, reported:

*Rail service to Chilhowee at the time was a mixed passenger-freight* train scheduled for tri-weekly trips from Knoxville. Livestock often had to be coaxed off the tracks. Sometimes the train came out on Tuesday and 'tried all week to get back to Knoxville'. From Chilhowee, the only way to ride on to Calderwood was by two-horse spring wagon, called a hack, owned by Alcoa. But only six or eight people could ride in that. Many walked.

    Southern Railway's timetable for further construction on the line was not satisfactory so Alcoa built the sixteen miles of track needed to access their new headquarters and dam site and billed Southern for the work.
    The Tallasee Power Company, shortened to Tapoco Inc. in 1955, and their holdings had been purchased in 1914 by Alcoa. This subsidiary would construct and operate the new dams. The first dam, called Cheoah, was built on the Little T. just upstream from its confluence with the Cheoah River. With the arrival of the railroad at the dam site, a complete construction village, Cheoah, North Carolina later changed to Tapoco, North Carolina was built to facilitate a massive construction job deep in the wilderness of the Smokies.
    The 225 foot high and 750 foot long curved concrete gravity type dam and its resulting 595 acre reservoir was completed on April 13, 1919. The original powerhouse contained four 33,000 horsepower turbines fitted to four 21,053 kwh Allis-Chalmers generators. In 1949 a fifth generator was installed, to produce an average annual generation of 515,600,000 kwh of electrical power. When the Cheoah project was completed, it was the highest overflow dam and housed the largest hydroelectric generating units in the world. (Cheoah Dam was used in the 1993 Warner Brothers movie *The Fugitive* starring Harrison Ford for the famous "jump off the dam" scene.) A 28-mile-long 161,000 volt transmission line was built across the mountains from the dam to the Alcoa aluminum works in Tennessee. From the Calderwood Dam overlook on U.S. Highway 129, one can see a single span of 5,010 feet. This span crossing Calderwood Lake from mountain to mountain was the longest single transmission line in the world for many years.
    Tapoco's next dam, the 212 foot high Santeetlah Dam—completed on June 7, 1928, on the Cheoah River—would claim more superlatives. During the construction of Santeetlah, the water-cement ratio to control concrete quality and mechanical vibrators

**Cheoah Dam, built 1919.**

to compact concrete were used for the first time on a large structure.

Even though the wooden hydroflume at the Ocoee #2 Dam, completed on the Ocoee River in 1913, preceded Santeetlah by 15 years, and hydro-conduits were used on a number of other mountain dams, the setup at Santeetlah is unique. The amount of electricity that can be made with a given volume of water varies directly with the "head." The head is defined by Webster as "the vertical distance between two points in a fluid"; some engineers have called it the height from which water falls to produce power. Specifically, in regard to hydroelectric production, it is the distance from the surface level of the reservoir to the level of the turbine. The higher the head, the more power produced from each gallon of water. If the powerhouse had been placed at the toe of Santeetlah Dam, a head of about 200 feet would have been available. But Tapoco engineers instead routed the water flow from the dam through a five mile long combination tunnel and pipeline across the mountains to the powerhouse placed on the banks of Cheoah Lake upstream from Cheoah Dam. This arrangement accomplished several things. First, the head was increased to 660 feet—the highest in the Eastern U.S. in 1928—allowing more than three times as much power to be generated with the same amount of water. Next, the discharge water, rather than being released back into the Cheoah River, where it would have entered the Little T. just below Cheoah Dam, was now released above Cheoah, giving the 371 cubic feet/second flow of water an extra turn at spinning the company's generators.

An interesting by-product of this river reroute was that the lower 12 miles of the Cheoah River was de-watered except for tributaries below the dam. During the first half of the 20th Century, environmental awareness was limited and environmental activism almost unheard of. Sections of a number of rivers in mountainous areas were rendered dry for the sake of kilowatts—rivers were to be controlled and utilized. Remember Congressman Joe Cannon's sentiment "not one cent for scenery." Imagine the uproar if someone today proposed to remove the water from a pristine whitewater river so that a private company could make their product more cheaply.

**Modern pot line in 1953.**

ALCOA

After 63 years of continuous service, the old wooden hydroflume at Ocoee #2 was taken out of service to be rebuilt in 1976. According to Charles Tichy, TVA historic architect, even though the five mile long structure anchored high on the side of the Ocoee River gorge had been placed on the National Register of Historic Places, and much hoopla was made that the flume should be restored as original, it was TVA engineering studies that determined that the most practical and economical method of repair was to follow original construction plans. During the years this tedious construction job was underway, the natural flow of the river was returned to the riverbed and very quickly commercial whitewater outfitters began operating on the river. By the early 1980's, with flume repair almost complete, TVA prepared to once again de-water the river. Commercial outfitters and private paddlers wrote letters, signed petitions, sought media coverage, and generally raised hell. Since the Ocoee is Tennessee's only real whitewater river, the state's travel and tourism authorities also jumped on the band wagon. The result was that Congress mandated that 116 days of recreational water releases would be provided by TVA annually and that commercial outfitters would pay TVA a per person fee to recoup electrical revenues lost.

In late 1998, Tapoco Inc. initiated studies and public hearings to prepare for the relicensing by the Federal Energy Regulatory Commission of Santeetlah Dam in 2003. A few respondents have called for the removal of the dam but a large contingent comprised of environmental groups, paddlers, and local business interests are asking for recreational water releases. I have seen the river several times during floods when gates at the dam were opened and the water allowed to run the original channel—it is awesome.

Two other subsidiaries were formed by Alcoa to effect company president Arthur V. Davis' plan to develop the entire Little T. and its tributaries for hydro power. The Carolina Aluminum Company was formed to purchase and hold lands for future hydro development. On July 23, 1929, Nantahala Power and Light Company was formed as a public utility to develop, construct, and operate dams on the upper Little T. and its tributaries. NP& L would eventually build and operate a total of 15 dams, including Nantahala—the first large hydro dam to utilize rock and earth fill construction—and my personal favorite, Diamond Valley, called a vest-pocket dam at six feet high and 12 feet long it diverts enough water to generate a million kilowatt hours each year. If a dam can be cute, Diamond Valley is it. Purchased by Duke Power Company in 1988, NP&L today serves 60,000 households and businesses in five western North Carolina counties.

Prior to 1933, Alcoa through its subsidiary Carolina Aluminum Company had purchased many tracts of land totaling just over 15,000 acres from the upstream end of Cheoah Reservoir to near the old town of Bushnell—located at the confluence of the Little T. and the Tuckasegee—for the purpose of constructing their next stairstep dam and reservoir on the Little Tennessee.

The unemployed 22 year old, Charles Martin Hall, had set in motion a chain of events that resulted in the first hydroelectric developments on the Little Tennessee River. A man of much different background and station in life would be the catalyst to continue the metamorphosis of the Fontana Area—the 32nd president of the United States, Franklin Delano Roosevelt.

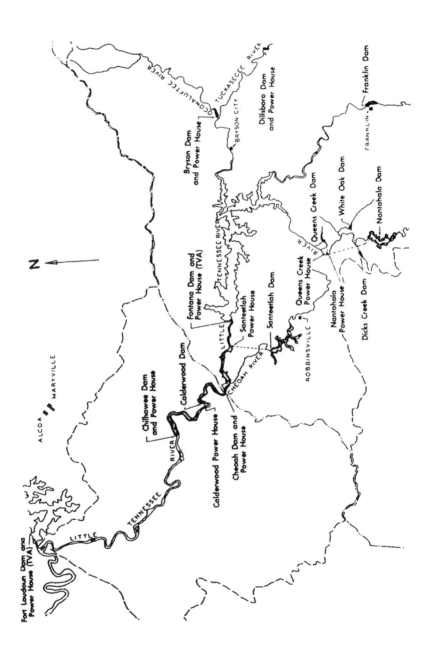

**Hydro-electric developments in the Little Tennessee watershed.**

Chapter 10

# Dreamers with Shovels

The Great Depression was gripping America when Franklin Roosevelt was inaugurated in March of 1933. During the first 100 days of his administration, Roosevelt rammed through Congress a number of social and domestic programs that would be collectively known as the New Deal. Just days into his first term, in a speech at Muscle Shoals, Alabama, he proclaimed, "The Muscle Shoals development and the Tennessee River development as a whole are national in their aspect and are going to be treated from a national point of view." The Tennessee Valley Authority (TVA) was created by Act of Congress on May 18, 1933. The new agency, operating in a 40,000 square mile area in seven states, would be the first real attempt at regional planning in the United States. In fact, Roosevelt viewed TVA as the working model for a national planning agency.

To achieve the unified development of the region's resources, TVA's objectives as directed by Congress, were:

*1) Effective water control on the Tennessee River and substantial assistance to flood control on the lower Ohio and Mississippi Rivers.*

*2) Development of navigation on the Tennessee River, linking the region to the Nation's 9000-mile system of improved interconnected inland waterways.*

*3) Widespread and abundant use of electric power.*

TVA

**The narrows of the Little Tennessee River—site of Fontana Dam.**

4) Greater opportunities for agriculture, industry, and forestry production.

5) Development and introduction of more efficient soil fertilizers.

Many of the country's best young engineers flocked to the new agency, including Wylie Bowmaster, who years later recalled: "This was totally new to develop a whole river in order to get the most you could out of that river. Our job was to get the most out: first for flood control, second for navigation and third for power. You could build a system to do any one of those three or to do two of them, but to do three of them and balance them out economically, that was the trick." To perform the trick, TVA would eventually build or buy nine main stream dams with navigation locks on the Tennessee River itself and 17 high dams on tributary streams.

The Little Tennessee River—with its three Alcoa dams and a complete development plan already in place at the creation of TVA—was a major piece in the puzzle of total river system development. Negotiations between Alcoa and TVA began almost immediately. Since Alcoa was in the aluminum business rather than the electric business, they were receptive to selling all or part of their electrical interests to TVA and being paid with a dependable stream of electrical current. Shortfalls in Congressional appropriations, changing priorities, and the expiration of TVA's authorization to pay for dam and reservoir properties with electric power resulted in the discontinuance of negotiations on June 2, 1936, by action of the TVA Board of Directors.

Over the next four years, while Alcoa completed Nantahala and Glenville dams on Little T. tributaries, and TVA wallowed in political infighting between its social visionary chairman, renowned hydraulic engineer Arthur Morgan, and its pragmatic self-important director, Harvard educated lawyer, David Lillienthal, neither the company nor the government directed much effort toward the Fontana Dam site. By early 1940, growing war clouds and a general increase in aluminum usage for everything from teapots to airplanes had caused demand to outstrip supply. Alcoa applied to the Federal Power Commission for a permit to construct Fontana Dam subject to TVA approval. The commission granted the permit but ruled the company would also need a license giving the government certain rights to reclaim the project after 50 years. Opinion No. 61 of the Federal Power Commission stated that "On November 5, 1940, the Commission found that the interests of interstate commerce would be substantially affected by the construction and operation of the project, indicating that a license would be required under the Federal Power Act."

This determination seemed a bit bogus to the Alcoa officials since there were already two high dams with no locks downstream of the Fontana Dam site. J.E.S. Thorpe, President of Nantahala Power and Light Company said that "The proposed Fontana Dam was to be built on the Little Tennessee River in the mountains of western North Carolina more than 20 miles above any known navigation. Greatly to our surprise the Federal Power Commission found that interstate commerce would be affected." One might wonder if this road block was a trump card played by the government to encourage Alcoa to relinquish the dam site to TVA. David Lillienthal, by then TVA chairman after Roosevelt fired Arthur Morgan, was well known for his legal maneuvering. Editorials in the Asheville Citizen-Times newspaper reflected reservations:

> The Citizen has read with lively interest and some wonderment the complete text of the ruling which the Federal Power Commission issued

*in this case. To state it mildly, the reasoning to which the Commission resorts in justifying its assumption of jurisdiction over the Little Tennessee River is so thin in spots as to be positively threadbare… The Citizen hopes that the Federal Power Commission will be as active in encouraging this development by government enterprise as it has been successful in discouraging its construction by private enterprise.*

The U.S. Supreme Court heard the case in the summer of 1940 and decided in U.S. vs Appalachian Power Company (another Alcoa subsidiary) that the Little Tennessee River and the proposed Fontana Lake are navigable. The Code of Federal Regulations defines "navigable waters of the United States" and "navigable waters" applicable to this case as "Internal waters of the United States not subject to tidal influence that are or have been used, or are or have been susceptible for use, by themselves or in connection with other waters, as highways for substantial interstate or foreign commerce, notwithstanding natural or manmade obstructions that require portage." Much of the Federal Power Commission's case for navigability was based on the operation of Kitchen Lumber Company's steamboat the *Vivian* in the 1920's. Lucille Boyden in her book *Village of Five Lives* wrote "This company initiated the use of a large, homemade steamboat on the Little Tennessee, as a unique means here of transporting enormous quantities of lumber to a contact point with Southern Railroad at the town of Fontana." The town of Fontana was located at the confluence of Eagle Creek and the Little T. about one mile upstream from the proposed dam site. Carson and Alberta Brewer reiterated the story in *Valley So Wild*:

*There are isolated incidents of river navigability in the mountain areas. Notable among them is the story of the Vivian which operated in the 1920's on a few miles of the Little Tennessee from near the present Fontana rock quarry to where the Southern Railway line ended at the old lumber town of Fontana (now under the lake).*

Fontana Lake is still classified as commercially navigable today. In 1995, I was involved in challenging the navigability of the lake on behalf of Fontana Village Resort due to exorbitant cost increases of operating commercial boat shuttles and tours in compliance with U.S. Coast Guard regulations for such navigable waters. My investigation of the situation revealed some interesting facts. I examined Kitchen Lumber Company and Southern Railway records, interviewed and corresponded with John R. Kitchen, son of company co-founder James H. Kitchen, and interviewed and visited the site with Burlin Green, area historian whose father helped build the *Vivian*. This research revealed that the first step in Kitchen's lumbering operation was to construct a three mile railroad from the town of Fontana down the Little T. past the future Fontana Dam site to the company's town, Kitchensville, located near where the huge rock quarry for the construction of the dam is today. A railroad spur was also built from Kitchensville on downriver for about one-half mile to their sawmill. All sawn lumber was taken to Fontana and all supplies were brought in via this railroad.

Furthermore, Whiting Manufacturing Company built a logging railroad around Welch and Lewellyn coves in the 1920's. This road connected to the line from Fontana to Kitchensville via a temporary low-water bridge across the river about one-half mile upstream from Kitchensville. Both of these railroads were removed at the conclusion of the logging operations in the 1930's.

The *Vivian* and her barges were only used on the waters of Cheoah Lake to transport logs and supplies between the sawmill and the logging operations on Twenty Mile Creek and other streams that emptied into the lake. Only occasionally, when the lake was high, was the *Vivian* able to make it up to the commissary dock at Kitchensville. Occasionally, personnel would be transported by boat down Cheoah Lake to connect with Alcoa's railroad at Tapoco, North Carolina. Both Mr. Kitchen and Mr. Green stated that the *Vivian* never attempted to go upstream past Kitchensville. An examination of the riverbed today between the quarry and the dam will reveal heavy shoaling that prevents the passage of all but very shallow draft fishing boats.

The potential for commercial barge traffic did exist on Fontana Lake after its construction from the Fontana Copper Mine, which became isolated on the north shore of the lake. The mine property was purchased and made a part of the Great Smoky Mountains National Park on June 9, 1983, thus ending the potential of commercial navigation. All of this "evidence" was presented to the U.S. Coast Guard for a determination. My efforts to refute the navigability of these waters was no more successful than Alcoa's—they lost their court case, and my appeal was denied. Fontana Lake is still classified as commercially navigable.

Even though much mud had been slung by both the government and Alcoa, the impending war crisis evidently encouraged reconciliation. Years later an Alcoa publication reported "The governmental agency and the private company interested in power for aluminum-making have been pointed to as a model of the way government and industry can sometimes work in harmony for the mutual benefit of each." *The Fontana Project*, TVA's official record of the work states:

> *The Fontana Agreement, as the contract between the Aluminum Co. of America and the TVA is commonly called, is a milestone in the relations between government and business. For the first time in the history of the United States a privately owned generating system was to be regulated by a public agency on the basis of an agreement arrived at by negotiation.*

Although aluminum production was the primary "war effort" objective and certainly the publicized purpose for Fontana Dam, TVA would be required to furnish vast amounts of electric power to another super-secret wartime project.

The completion of Fontana would occur at such a time that its "contribution would be significant in the closing stages of the war." Just west of Knoxville a city for 75,000 people was built surrounded by a high fence—armed guards, some with machine guns, patrolled the perimeter. Inside the fence would be built huge factories. Only a few dozen people living there knew the purpose of the project. One displaced local observed that "Everything in the world goes in there but nothing ever comes out." Finally in mid-1945, a small quantity of the product, U-235, was secretly shipped from the facility. The material became the primary ingredient for the world's first use of atomic energy as a military weapon—the bomb that leveled Hiroshima on August 6, 1945. The secret city was called Oak Ridge.

The Fontana Agreement was signed on August 14, 1941, and is summarized in *The Fontana Project* as follows:

> *The Aluminum Co. transferred to TVA title to all property it had acquired for the Fontana project, amounting to 400 separate tracts ag-*

gregating nearly 15,000 acres. For this property TVA gave no cash consideration but, instead, waived any claim under section 10 of the Federal Power Act or otherwise to compensation for the benefits resulting to Alcoa's Cheoah and Calderwood projects from headwater regulation by the Fontana project. Conveyance of property was to be effected immediately upon the appropriation of funds to TVA for construction of the project. In the event Congress did not make the necessary appropriation for construction of Fontana by September 30, 1942, the agreement could be canceled by either party. Beginning with completion of the Fontana project, TVA was given the right to direct the impounding and release of water at all of the company's plants in the Little Tennessee Basin and to take all power generated at Alcoa plants in the TVA system, returning dump power to the company immediately, and making available within each year an amount of power equal to the amount of power other than dump power obtained from the company's plants. For the right to direct the Alcoa generating plants, and thus realize substantial advantages to its own plants on the main stem of the Tennessee River, TVA was obligated to furnish the company with 11,000 kilowatts of primary power.

Funding to begin construction was included in the Third Supplemental National Defense Appropriation Bill for 1942. The bill passed Congress on December 16, 1941, and was signed into law by President Roosevelt the next day. Construction began on January 1, 1942.

As time passed, each resource developer that came into the Fontana area could build on the transportation links constructed by their predecessors. The existing roads in the area provided at least rudimentary access to the project site but were severely insufficient to support such a massive effort. The Construction and Maintenance Division of TVA was responsible for building the support facilities for actual dam construction. The introduction of the C&M Division's "Final Cost Report" provides a good picture of the situation:

*Fontana Dam, one of the Authority's largest war-time rush projects, was started in mid-winter, January 1942. The dam site is an isolated mountainous location on the upper reaches of the Little Tennessee River near the North Carolina-Tennessee State line about 10 miles east of Deals Gap in Swain-Graham Counties, North Carolina. This project had* all the elements of a difficult job. There was no adequate access by road, no housing for workmen, no near communities of any size, a sparsely populated mountain country with no close skilled or unskilled labor, no telephone, telegraph or power lines and, coupled with these items, a tight time schedule for dam completion. The Authority's C&M Division, a unit of the Engineering and Construction Department, was assigned the work of constructing an Access Road, a Camp for workmen, a Village for workmen and operators, together with other miscellaneous jobs incident to the opening up of a project of this size.

Access to the project by road in the beginning was by way of Deals Gap on the Tennessee-North Carolina line where Tennessee Highway No. 61 joins North Carolina Highway No. 129, thence over a narrow, winding, low grade mountain road, North Carolina Temporary No. 288, for a distance of approximately 10 miles, then off the road into the job site a distance of 1 1/2 miles over an abandoned logging railroad bed. From Deals Gap back to Maryville, Tennessee is a distance of approximately 35 miles, or from Deals Gap back to Robbinsville, North Carolina, a distance of approximately 30 miles, both over fair black top mountain roads. From the dam site to Bryson City, North Carolina, the distance was approximately 35 miles by way of temporary North Carolina No. 288, an extremely narrow, winding mountain road, totally unsuited for heavy hauling and personnel traffic.

A rail head and an old light duty logging railroad did exist into what was known as Fontana Station. This was approximately one mile east of the dam site, upstream, and was the end of a branch line from Bushnell, North Carolina off the Asheville-Murphy Line of the Southern Railway. By rail from Fontana Station back to Bryson, City, North Carolina was a distance of approximately 26 miles.

Fontana rail head and highway access were both located on the north or right bank of the Little Tennessee River, whereas the proposed camp and village were located on the left bank, or the south side of the river some 2 miles inland and up some 800 ft.

Despite winter weather, poor transportation and extremely rough living conditions incident to the project location, construction was rushed on all phases of the preliminary work. For the first group of men working on the project, a temporary tent camp (approximately 85 tents) was set up, temporary construction shacks built, a wash house and a temporary mess hall, which were located on the north bank of the river near the Fontana rail head. An old ferry of very light capacity was pressed into service and job area construction roads were started. Heavy

**River ferry.**

road equipment was brought in and work started on the dam access road, beginning at the dam site and moving back towards Deals Gap. Concurrently, camp site grading for the permanent camp was started and building materials began to roll into the rail head by rail. As soon as a rough construction road could be opened up across the river from the rail head to the camp site, a distance of 1-1/4 miles, a heavy duty ferry was built and put into operation on a 24-hour basis. Men, materials, and equipment moved in on the camp site and immediate construction was started on all principal camp features. First, at the camp site, a second temporary tent camp for workmen was built, (approximately 100 tents) together with wash houses and temporary cafeteria. Following in close order came a temporary water supply, men's permanent dormitories, permanent camp cafeteria, permanent water and sewerage system, electric distribution system, telephone lines, roads, streets and other site grading. By June 1, 1942, or less than 6 months after the beginning of job, a complete camp for men had come into existence with all facilities to handle up to 2500 men. During this same time, *progress on the dam access road had reached the point where the road was opened to traffic half way between Deals Gap and the dam site, or a distance of approximately 5 miles over the new grade with only 5 miles left to be covered over the old road (NC 288).*

It is interesting to note that NC Highway 288 is referred to as "temporary" in this report; however, at the time of the highway's construction it was certainly not thought of as being temporary. Swain County and the state of North Carolina knew of Alcoa's plans to build two dams between the head of Cheoah Lake and Bryson City that would flood the railroad and old turnpike that ran along the river. To provide future access to the towns and settlements located on the north side of the river, a road bond was passed to fund the construction of the new Hwy. 288 that would be built high enough on the mountain side to avoid flooding by Alcoa's 200 foot high dam at Fontana. TVA's 480-foot high dam did

**North Carolina Highway 288.**

COURTESY OF GSMNP

**Construction tent camp #1.**

flood sections of the road so that in 1945, when the C&M report was written, NC Hwy. 288 had indeed become temporary. The flooding of this road and subsequent loss of access would become a major controversy that has still not been settled over 50 years later.

One veteran carpenter would describe the Fontana project to TVA Chairman David Lillienthal as "One hell of a big job of work." The first tent camp was located at the confluence of Payne Branch and the Little Tennessee (now under the lake). Throughout most of the project, housing needs lagged far behind availability. W.N. Rogers, TVA Personnel Officer, reported:

> As we approach the final stages of the Construction and Maintenance phase of the Fontana Project, we can reflect back over the past two years and see the major problems encountered from a personnel viewpoint, can indicate the approach made and evaluate the results in terms of a magnificent job done by the C&M Division, showing results of complete cooperation between the Personnel Division and the C&M Division.
> From the very beginning of the project, almost every known type

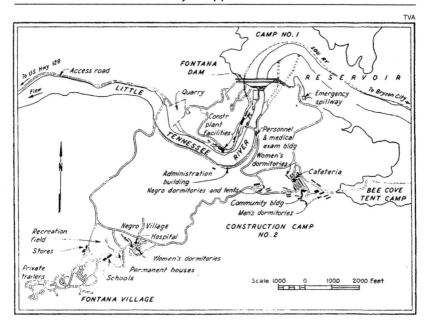

**General layout of Fontana village and Construction Camp.**

of labor problem was confronted, and chief among these were recruitment problems, absenteeism, and labor turnover.

Fontana had been approved as a war effort project on an almost unbelievable schedule. In little more than six months it was necessary to construct a camp with fifteen large dormitories, cafeteria, community building, and numerous other buildings, and also to construct a village with several hundred houses, two school buildings, a food store, and a community center. Add to this the construction of miles of paved roads that had to be blasted foot by foot from the mountain sides and one begins to picture the Herculean task that was completed in record time.

The recruitment of labor has been most difficult from the start due to the limited number of laborers in the Fontana area, and this is especially true of the thirty-five mile area around the dam which is usually considered the commuting area. Also, the construction of Fontana was unattractive to most people outside the commuting area because of the inaccessibility of the project. Conditions were aggravated by the fact that work on the dam was started approximately the same time as the C&M began, creating deplorable living conditions. A small tent camp was put up, with a cafeteria much too small to care for the large number whose very existence depended upon it. Hundreds slept in cars, in temporary shacks, in culverts, and under trees. It was July of 1942 before sleeping quarters were made available to unskilled labor. This created the first problem in recruitment in that laborers resigning from the job spread the information over the entire area about living conditions at Fontana, probably resulting in the refusal of hundreds and hundreds who otherwise would have accepted work.

The second tent camp was located in a narrow cove just northwest of the present location of the Fontana Riding Stable. The construction camp was located between where the Stable and Swim Club are today, near the intersection of N.C. 28 and the road to the top of the dam. After Fontana Village was turned into a resort, this area was the site of the old Par 3 Golf Course for many years. The camp area was known as Gold Branch Cove prior to TVA's arrival and was the location of the one room Welch Cove School in addition to several houses. The construction camp consisted of 11 large dormitories for single men and three for single women.

The 15,000 square foot community building that housed a

**Some of the first workers slept in large culverts.**

TVA

**Main construction camp for single workers.**

movie theater/auditorium, class rooms, library, commissary, fire department and post office was the anchor piece for the surrounding recreational facilities, including softball fields, horseshoe pits, and a pool hall. Ironically, during the VJ Day celebration (victory in Japan), a drunken fireman set the building on fire, causing considerable damage. These facilities—like everything at Fontana during the dam construction period—operated 24 hours per day, seven days a week to accommodate workers on all three shifts. To help combat labor turnover and keep morale high, much effort was put into recreational activities. Project Manager Fred C. Schlemmer often said that "contented workers equal concrete."

One of the main ways to keep the work force happy was to feed them well. The project cafeteria, also located at the construction camp, exceeded at this Herculean task. R.H. Couch, cafeteria manager, kept a scrap book that reveals much about the scope of the task and the success of the operation. The total number of meals served in May of 1943 was 182,640 or almost 6,000 per day. The cafeteria operated around the clock with meal times set by shift changes. In addition, the cafeteria's "Sandwich Factory" prepared over 2,000 sack lunches each day for consumption on the job site. To accomplish all this, in a single month the staff prepared 21,533 pounds of meat, 10,951 pounds of poultry, 6,800 pounds of fish, 20,190 dozen eggs, 42,800 pounds of potatoes and assorted other ingredients, totaling over 128 tons of food procured, processed, and prepared. Procurement of food stuffs was sometimes the hardest part of the process with war time shortages and rationing. Special agents were sent out to "encourage" suppliers to route supplies to the project. In a letter praising Mr. Couch and his staff for the wonderful food prepared for "the men and women who are building Fontana Dam," Project Manager Schlemmer, closing with his usual patriotic zeal, wrote that "… for they are the soldiers of the home front, supporting the men in the service who are fighting and dying in order that we may eat in victory instead of starve in defeat."

Concurrently with the construction of the camp, a complete town was built two miles away in Welch Cove. Today known as Fontana Village, Welch Cove was the home to six hardy farm fami-

**Fontana construction camp community building.**

TVA

lies when TVA officials first arrived. TVA's January 1942 acquisition map reveals that half the houses were log and only a rough wagon trail connected the cove to the outside world. Jessie Gunter's one and a half story log house, the cemetery where his wife and children are buried, and scattered craggy old apple trees, remnants of once proud orchards, are about all that is left to remind us of the cove's pioneer heritage.

Housing for workers with families was provided by constructing 25 permanent houses, 62 temporary single houses, 93 temporary duplex houses, 100 demountable houses, and 104 trailer houses. In addition, TVA owned trailers and parking for privately owned trailers were also provided. The permanent and temporary houses were stick-built on site and utilized much lumber that was salvaged from reservoir clearing. I live in a Fontana house that I moved to my farm and remodeled. Part of the house is framed with American chestnut that had succumbed to the chestnut blight in the middle 1930's and was plentiful around Fontana.

**Fontana Dam Cafeteria, the sign over the door reads "Work! or Fight!"**

TVA

**Fontana Village, 1943.**

The stick-built houses were constructed using a new assembly line technique that would revolutionize single home construction in America after the war when tens of thousands of tract houses were built in a very short time. The C&M Cost Report describes the process:

*In house construction, line production was used as much as possible and resulted in completion of as many as 3 houses per day. One labor crew excavated for foundations and dug water and sewer trenches to street connection. Masons followed and put in foundations and part way up on the chimney. A carpenter crew framed in the houses and put on the siding. A roofing crew placed roofing. Another carpenter crew installed floors, interior wallboard and trim. At proper intervals, plumbing was roughed in and electrical material was placed. As soon as siding was placed, painting crews followed with the prime coat and followed through with finishing costs. Tinners placed guttering, chimney flashing and other metal parts. A labor crew followed for yard clean-up and dress-up.*

House types were allocated by job classification with the best houses going to upper management. Many of the best, permanent type houses were on Fontana Road, which runs along the top of a ridge in the center of the village. This street had many nicknames: Snob Knob, Fuzzy Dog Row, and Silk Stocking Row (only the most affluent ladies could afford silk stockings). The temporary houses were well built but had wood post foundations. Many of these houses have been remodeled several times and still serve as rental cottages at Fontana Village.

The demountable and trailer houses were similar in appearance, layout, and portability. The demountables were originally constructed and used at a nitrate plant in Sheffield, Alabama. Most were sent to the Hiawasse Project near Murphy, North Carolina before arriving at Fontana. These two or four cell units were built with standard frame construction materials, 2x framing and 1x siding. Each 7'6" x 32' cell was complete with wiring, plumbing, and some built-in cabinetry. The cells were fitted with rollers underneath so that when they arrived at their prepared wood post foundations they could be rolled off the truck-pulled trailers along pipe rail tracks into position and be bolted to their matching half, forming a complete one bedroom cottage. The 4-cell models were basically two, 2-cell units assembled side by side to create a three bedroom, two bath home. A small crew using ropes, pulleys, and support poles could unload, position, connect, and finish a demountable or trailer house in a matter of hours. There are stories of workers literally standing in the street, luggage in hand, waiting for their house to be set up so they could throw their stuff inside and report to work.

The design and manufacture of the trailer or prefabricated house is a story in itself. Designated as the A-6, they were the forerunner of the modern double-wide. TVA Chief Architect Roland

***The telephone switchboard at Fontana Village, 1943.***

**Type A-6 cottage.**

Wank and world renowned architect Albert Kahn had collaborated early in TVA history, probably spurred by the Utopian visions of TVA's first chairman, Arthur Morgan. The cemesto house used at Norris Dam, line production of stick built houses, and the possibility of prefabricated houses for the masses led to the practical application of some radical new ideas. Kahn had become famous for his approach to assembly-line factory designs at Henry Ford's automobile plants at Highland Park and Rouge River near Detroit in the late teens and early twenties. He created a factory design that allowed a continuous flow from raw material to finished product. Kahn also designed such noteworthy structures as the French Museum of Art.

    The two architects believed that assembly line techniques coupled with aircraft type lightweight design could produce an inexpensive, semi-portable, yet comfortable housing unit. The result was the A-6. These houses were built by Schultz Trailers, Inc. of Eckhart, Indiana according to previously prepared TVA plans and specifications. The structure was basically a stress skin covering of thin plywood glued to a lightweight balloon frame of minimal dimension lumber. Plywood and cardboard joists provided floor and roof support. All wiring, plumbing, fixtures, cabinetry, and furnishing were installed at the factory. The two-cell A-6 houses were transported and set-up in the same fashion as the demountable houses but much easier and quicker due to their light weight and less on site finishing.

One hundred and four of these units were placed at Fontana. Over the years, as the TVA houses at Fontana were remodeled for resort use, the A-6 did not receive much attention. Their unconventional construction did not lend itself to easy modification so they were rented to the tourists in close to original condition and were the bargain basement of accommodations at the resort. A sort of a cult following grew for the little inexpensive one bedroom units. I have talked to many parents who brought their children to stay in one of the little cabins they had stayed in on mountain vacations in their childhood. People used the inside of the desk drawer as a guest comment registry recording dates and high points of their visit. One entry read "Stayed in this cabin in July 1961 when I was 10 years old, there was a mouse under the sink. Have brought my kids in June 1976, the mouse's descendants are still here."

A major lodging renovation occurred at Fontana in the late 1980's and early 1990's. Many of the A-6's were sold and removed to make room for new units; dozens of the little cabins are scat-

# Dreamers With Shovels 151

*Interiors and plans for the Type A-6 cottage (opposite and this page).*

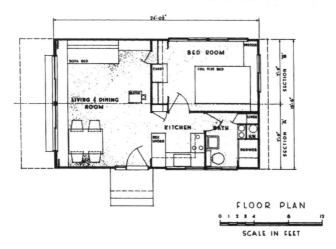

tered around western North Carolina today. During this period the University of Connecticut School of Architecture was doing research on the work of Albert Kahn. Staff member Elizabeth Grossman was dispatched to see if she could discover any of the work Kahn did for TVA. After a protracted and arduous search, she finally linked up with TVA historic architect Charles Tichy, who sent her to me—suggesting that she had better hurry. The following day she sat down in my office and told of her mission and the ordeal she had been through. Ms. Grossman then produced a photocopy of a page from the November 1945 French architectural journal "Techniques Et Architecture." The page contained a photograph of an A-6, one half in place and the other half being backed into position behind a late 30's International pickup truck. The caption read "TVA Shulte Trailer House. Albert Kahn Architect." She asked "Have you ever seen anything that looks like that?" I said "Yes ma'am, that's 522, it's right up above the cafeteria, ya wanna see it?"

She was elated. That afternoon we visited, photographed, measured, and generally enjoyed a number of the remaining A-6 houses. Elizabeth would gleefully point out Kahnish architectural nuances. Also, that afternoon, I became a member of the Cult of

**Fontana Village Type A-6 cottage #522. From Techniques et Architecture, 1945, "TVA Shulte Trailer House, Albert Kahn architecte."**

the A-6. At the dawn of the 21st Century, only six of the sturdy little houses remain at Fontana. They are no longer rented to the public and hopefully someday will be restored into a small historic district.

*Chapter 11*
# Work or Fight

Almost all Americans who lived through World War II have vivid memories of the time, whether they were on the beach at Normandy, shot down over the Pacific, living in New York City, or in the backwoods of Appalachia. The transition from the Great Depression to the war years must have been a heady experience. A study of the lifestyle in a government war project hidden deep in the wilderness of the Smoky Mountains reveals much about the times.

Several service facilities were constructed to complete the little city of Fontana Village in Welch Cove. Located in the center of the village, the elementary and high schools were the most prominent of the public buildings. The schools contained a total of 19 classrooms, a large auditorium ( also used as a movie theater, as well as for church services and civic functions by the community), and an adjacent manual training shop. Project Manager Fred Schlemmer wrote that "The Fontana Schools were perhaps the most important single factor in the development of contentment and satisfaction among the employee-residents of the community." Over 600 students hailing from 46 of the then 48 states attended classes here between 1942 and 1946. This was a very special small window of time in the lives of these young people who scattered like the wind as their parents moved on to other jobs.

In the mid-1980's two alumni, Doris Couch Clayton and Eloise Barton Brock—who had occasionally vacationed at Fontana—got together and decided to try and find enough of their fellow "Dam Kids" to have a school reunion. They would eventually locate sev-

**School Buildings, later converted to house the Recreational Hall.**

eral hundred classmates and even a few "Dam Teachers," too. The first reunion was held October 4-5, 1986. On the morning of the 4th, I was preparing to lead a nature hike at the trailhead on the west side of the dam when two of the former students, Nelson Seaman and Harvey Welch, emerged from a side trail and asked if I could get help for an elderly man down the trail who had broken his leg. As I mobilized a rescue, I struck up a conversation with these two good Samaritans. That chance meeting led to a long and enjoyable relationship with the former students—my wife, Tina, and I were even made honorary Dam Kids at a later reunion.

The reminiscence of these folks have been invaluable in trying to reconstruct what life was like in wartime Fontana. Eloise Barton Brock remembered:

> Coming from an area where my parents had grown up and lived all their lives, Fontana was a new experience to all of us. We kids had never moved from that area and were thrown with lots of other kids from lots of other places. I think army camps and defense jobs of that era began the real mobility of our country, and it was very educational and enlightening to meet others from all over the United States. Also,

coming from a rural area, with no inside plumbing and with homes that were less than comfortably warm at times, these new homes at Fontana with good insulation, indoor plumbing, electric stoves, etc. were somewhat a luxury to us. So, despite the crowded home and the hectic pace of both parents, we still felt we were very fortunate to live in such a well-kept village. I think the time (wartime when our nation was at risk), the place (an isolated mountain area separated from the rest of the world), and the people (from all over the United States and from all kinds of backgrounds) made Fontana the family-feeling which seemed to be felt by all. We didn't see strangers; just people we had not met. We felt safe on the streets at night; we could be picked up in cars by unknown neighbors without feeling any apprehension; the sound of the mounted police in the night gave us the feeling of protection and security. The fact that all families were engaged in what was considered an essential project, helping the war effort, made us all feel one family, united in one cause. As far as I was able to tell, there was no class distinction...we all were there for one reason, to build the dam as quickly and as safely as possible.

**Fontana High School students, 1943-1944.**

Eloise's sister Dorothy Barton Chewning summed up her experience with "Fontana is an emotion." Jimmy Marsh remembered some of the more colorful events—seems that Phil Rucker brought a funnel, a dime, and a bottle of water to school one day. The trick was to stick the funnel into the front of your pants, lean your head back, place the dime on your forehead and try to drop the dime into the funnel. Of course, while the unsuspecting player's head was leaned back, Rucker would produce the hidden bottle of water and flood the funnel. Then a dare went out to challenge Ms. Rogers, their teacher, to play—most were amused, but not Ms. Rogers. Not only Mr. Rucker and his equipment, but also several of the spectators made a visit to Mrs. McCall, the principal, that day.

A shopping center was built to serve the community. A combination grocery store, meat market, and dry goods store was on the south end of the complex and is still used today as the resort cafeteria. The other main building housed a drug store and soda fountain, the post office, a bank, and a beauty parlor. A small barber shop was built between the two main buildings. The drug

**Village Shopping center, 1945.**

TVA

Work or Fight  **159**

***Negro tent camp.***

store building remained in service until the early 1980's, its soda fountain being a gathering place for young resort guests just as it had been for the Dam Kids. During the summer of 1944, several of the boys noticed a farmer would arrive in the parking lot around dark several days per week with a load of watermelons on his flat bed truck. Even though the stores were open 24 hours per day, deliveries were only accepted during the day shift—so the farmer would spend the night in his truck. The boys soon started liberating a few watermelons each night the truck was in the parking lot. This went on for several weeks and some of the boys were convinced the farmer had seen them but did nothing to stop their undercover operation. Finally one night as the boys approached the truck, they found the truck surrounded by TVA Public Safety officers. Seems the old man had a little undercover operation of his own. Under the tarp the watermelons rested on was the real commodity—moonshine whiskey. This explained the farmer's disregard of the boy's pilfering, he didn't want to call attention to his operation.

An automobile service station was located down the street

**The hospital, now used for Village registration and administration.**

from the shopping center to accommodate resident's automotive needs. In the summer of 1943, due to the crowded conditions in the school buildings, the two story Red Cross building was constructed up Welch Road from the shopping center. The lower floor contained a minister's office and meeting rooms for the Boy and Girl Scouts. The upper floor housed the Red Cross operation. This building would later house the resort medical staff on the first floor and "The Lady of the Lake" Catholic chapel on the second.

In the 1940's, segregation was the law of the land. Black workers were actively recruited and made a major contribution to the success of the project. Separate housing, dining, and recreational facilities were constructed for their use. A school for black children was built across the highway from the hospital. The permanent visitor's building at the top of the dam was originally constructed with "colored" restrooms. Later, when segregation laws were changed, these restrooms were remodeled into shower rooms for use by Appalachian Trail hikers.

The medical needs of the project were fulfilled by a modern 50 bed hospital constructed on the main road from the village to the camp. This building was transformed into the Fontana Lodge, accommodating many resort guests from 1947 until 1983. It is used today as the resort registration and administration building. Several women's dormitories were built near the hospital to house nurses and other single female workers.

War type games were popular with kids all over the country during World War II and especially the village kids. Jimmy Marsh, Clyde Merritt, and several others formed the Fontana Air Force, Bomber Division. Using a grapevine swing as an aircraft, the division dropped bombs on the enemy by swinging from a high bank with a rock between their knees, releasing the projectile to land in a bucket target. The young aviators became relatively proficient but their ordinance did not fly true, so Clyde Merritt's dad built them a realistic wooden bomb complete with pointy nose and tail fins. Accuracy improved quickly, so now distance became the challenge. Clyde decided to try for the Olympic record for grapevine bomb tossing. He went farther up the start-hill than anyone had previously tried to begin his flight. As he flew through the air, with sort of a flipping move, he released the payload at just the perfect moment. According to reports, the bomb was still gaining altitude when it soared past the bucket. A hush fell over the crowd when the missile penetrated the roof of Clyde's house, sending its occupants scurrying outside to see what happened. At the insistence of Clyde's parents, the Air Force was disbanded. The boys soon reformed as ground troops. Fox holes and other earth works were built on the top of a high bank overlooking the hospital area. The young fellows busied themselves fighting the imaginary Japanese until the day Jimmy Hipps brought in a pair of binoculars, almost causing the boys to lose the war. As observations were made from their position it was discovered that they could clearly see through the windows of the nurses' dormitory. Somehow war games were no longer very exciting compared to visions of scantily clad nurses.

Life for the project's adults was probably not quite as much fun, but was equally fulfilling and memorable. The introduction to *Voices in the Valley: Remembering World War II* by TVA historian Mary Jane Lowe begins:

> "Built for the People of the United States." These words appear on the wall of every hydroelectric dam, fossil fuel steam plant, and nuclear

**A play in the community building.**

power plant built by the Tennessee Valley Authority (TVA). They embody the spirit of the agency. From its very inception and throughout its history TVA has responded to the needs of the Tennessee Valley and nation. This is especially true in times of crisis.

Almost all war industries suffered from labor shortages. The requirements of the Armed Service, coupled with the vast amount of work to be done, spread the labor force pretty thin. Fontana's remote location and, at least at first, Spartan facilities compounded the problem for the giant dam project. Workers were recruited with inviting booklets that touted the good living, food, recreation, and educational opportunities at the project. Project Manager Fred Schlemmer truly did believe that contented workers were more productive. In 1944 several elected officials, TVA senior managers, and members of the press toured the project. Mr. Alfred Mynders reported in the *Chattanooga Times:* "Before the tour, the group sat in Mr. Schlemmer's office. Mr. Brown said, 'So in this room is where the great dam is really built.' Quick as a flash, Mr. Schlemmer replied: 'No, the dam is really built back in our town where the workers live.'"

Even though this type of management attitude toward labor might have been scowled at by some industrialists as coddling the workers, the reality on the job site was not very soft. As a new employee approached the project, one of the first things he or she would see was a huge billboard depicting Uncle Sam declaring "If you want to work you're welcome at Fontana Dam. If you are a shirker we don't have time to fool with you." Other billboards were all around reminding workers that Fontana Dam was an essential war project, encouraging them to buy war bonds, and asking how many men will die in battle today because you laid out of work. The sign over the entrance to the cafeteria simply said "Work! or Fight!"

Fred Schlemmer could be thought of more as a head coach than an authoritative boss. He used numerous techniques and personae to encourage the work force toward maximum production. Regularly, Schlemmer would write reports that were posted on bulletin boards, printed in the weekly recreation bulletin, and handed out at worker meetings. These reports gave workers, spouses, and even the kids an ongoing play-by-play of specific construction progress along with a pep talk so that everyone felt part of the big picture. In a letter addressed "To the men and women who are building Fontana Dam" he wrote:

> Mr. Donald M. Nelson, Chairman of the War Production Board visited Fontana Dam on June 1 and 2. Mr. Nelson was very high in praise of the outstanding accomplishment made to date in the construction of Fontana Dam, by YOU, THE MEN AND WOMEN WHO ARE DOING THE JOB. He said that he was thrilled beyond words to see what is being done by an interested and patriotic group of American citizens who are proving that they understand the need for those at home to supply our fighting men with the things they need to WIN THE WAR. Mr. Nelson was greatly impressed with all that he saw, and with the evidence of the atmosphere of TEAMWORK which he observed. He was pleased with the cooperative understanding and relationship which exists between Labor and Management at Fontana Dam, and said that it was a fine example for the entire country to follow.

***Upstream face of dam during concrete placement.***

On another occasion Schlemmer described the present status of Fontana Dam in the employees' recreation bulletin:

> On everyone's lips is the expression of satisfaction in seeing our great dam rise higher toward the clouds with each succeeding day. Of course there are good reasons why it does. First, it is because this Fontana organization is working with all of its heart and might to show the world how one of the biggest jobs ever done is being prosecuted during a time when our country badly needs the maximum effort of every citizen.
>
> Up and up and up the concrete goes—every day more is added to prove that this Fontana outfit 'knows its stuff'. April with 211,000 yards, May with 244,000 yards, June with 236,000 yards—almost 700,000 yards of concrete in a three month period. That's something to be proud of. What will July's production be; that's a question which everyone is talking about.
>
> A novel idea has been developed for July. It's really a game. Management, by careful schedule has estimated what July's yardage should be—but has not made an announcement of its figure. Instead, the esti-

mated yardage figure has been placed under a locked cover on the concrete production board down on the job. Management has confidence that the men who are doing the job are setting their own schedule for this month. And there is no question but what it will be one of the best yet.

Schlemmer also took his message to the airwaves and revealed the theatric side of his personality and management style. A series of radio shows entitled "Fontana Goes to War" was broadcast on Asheville station WWNC, which could be picked up by Fontana residents as well as everybody else in the southern mountains who had a radio. An excerpt from the script of the May 20, 1943, episode broadcast at 9:45 p.m. E.W.T. (Eastern War Time) went like this:

**Schlemmer:** *Thank you Jim (announcer), and I want to introduce one of the men who are working night and day at Fontana to turn water into electricity for aluminum and planes—he is Hugh McShane, steamfitter and chairman of our union management War Production Drive Committee.*

**McShane:** *Thanks Mr. Schlemmer, I'm proud to be working on a 100% war job as long as I am part of the home front, but the man we want to hear is Lieut. Trice. He's been flying the planes that will be built with our power.*

**Lieut. Trice:** *You're right, Hugh, I've flown most of our fighter ships; Lancers, Warhawks, Lightnings, Airacobras and a good many more. Believe me, they are tops. We know where those planes are coming from, and we don't want anything—lack of ore, lack of metal, lack of man-power, lack of electric power—to stop them.*

**Schlemmer:** *Before we get too far tell us how you lost that leg, Lieutenant.*

At least once, Schlemmer's theatrics even went international. The Columbia Broadcasting System (CBS) in collaboration with the British Broadcasting Corporation (BBC) produced a radio program called "Transatlantic Call—People to People" in which "The people of the two countries tell their own stories." Episode Number 45 broadcast on Sunday, December 12, 1943, entitled "Dreamers with

Work or Fight  **167**

TVA

**Construction shops downstream from the dam, photo was taken from where the Visitor's Building is today.**

Shovels" featured Fontana. As the story unfolds, Alan Lomax, the narrator, is visiting the dam:

**Lomax:** *I stood on the highest trestle overlooking the works, nearly at a level with the tops of the hills all around. The half-completed dam spanned the narrow gorge below. The valley floor was swarming with men and machines. I could see where the black river disappeared into the diversion tunnels above the half-constructed dam; I could see the same river pouring out of the tunnel mouth below the dam…*

**Schlemmer:** *You see, Alan, what we're doing here is very simple. We're moving a mountain from one location down the river to another location here in the river channel.*

**Lomax:** *I see. Very simple.*

**Schlemmer:** *The whole idea is this. Crush a mountain into a suitable base for concrete. Move it a mile over and around a few other mountains. Mix with cement and pour. It's all done with conveyor belts…*

**Lomax:** *What do you like best about your job?*

**Schlemmer:** The people. The operations of Fontana are based on the precept that the dam is not being built in the channel of the river, but in the minds and hearts of the people who're building it. We believe that men—all men—desire to work. Our job is to provide them with good conditions under which to work and live out on this construction job…

**Lomax:** You mean you're concerned about morale…

**Schlemmer:** That's it. We've found, as a business proposition, that good morale is an important factor in the price of concrete…

**Lomax:** Suppose you could let me talk to some of the men on the job?

**Schlemmer:** Sure… Let's tackle this guy… He's a welder. Working on this steel tower here… Hi, Bud, how're you doin'?…

**Bud:** Not bad, not bad. We started this tower day before yesterday. The foreman figgers we'll top out tonight before we quit.

**Lomax:** For heaven's sake, that's fast. How tall is this tower?

**Bud:** Two hundred and ten feet.

**Schlemmer:** Show this gentleman where you're working, Bud…

**Bud:** Come on over here to the edge of the platform, mister…

**Lomax:** Now, wait a minute, I don't know whether I want to look over or not… It's a long way to the ground…

**Bud:** Don't look at the ground. Aw, come on… You're O.K… Now look where I'm pointing… See that plate there. I've got to put holes in it… Now, don't look down.

**Lomax:** You look down, Britain, and Bud's plate is about twenty feet below you; beneath that is nothing, emptiness, a two hundred foot drop to the base of the dam; down below, the figures of the men are like gnats crawling on the face of the rock…

**Bud:** Mister, don't look down. Don't be nervous, you're as safe here as you'd be in the office. Safer.

**Lomax:** Well, I don't feel as safe…

**Bud:** That's just what I mean. You think you're safe in an office. Here we know it's dangerous. That's why there are more accidents in offices than on high steel.

**Lomax:** Well, I don't see how you can stand to crawl down there and work right out over nothing at all…

**Bud:** Mister, more people died at home in bed last year than any other way. I ain't afraid to die in bed; so I'm not afraid to do my work out here… It's just as safe out here as you make it.

**Lomax:** Doesn't it make you dizzy to look at the ground?

**Bud:** I don't never see the ground. I look where I'm at and let the ground take care of itself…

**Lomax:** Well, I believe I'd rather have some other job…

**Bud:** Maybe you would. But I like mine…This dam's soon gonna be making planes for the war…I got a brother in there and he ain't got no family to fight for. I got a wife and a family and I figger if he can fight for himself, I can fight for them…

**Lomax:** How big a family, Bud?

**Bud:** Two little boys…And I want to help win this war before they take over so they won't have to do any fighting, so they'll be free…I know it's gonna take a lot of building and fighting to make this a decent world for my kids…

**Lomax:** Bud, you're terrific.

**Bud:** Nope. A guy's gotta work to eat. This is my job…But, looky here, if I don't get going the boss, here will think I talk more than I work…See you all later…

**Schlemmer:** O.K., Bud. Take it easy…

**Bud:** Sure (fading off very gradually) It's safer out here than in your hammock at home…Figger I'll make a welder out of my old lady next week. Have her hanging by her heels right alongside me…

**Schlemmer:** Watch him walk down that girder, just like he was climbing down a ladder…

**Lomax:** Marvelous.

Then on July 4, 1944, Schlemmer placed into operation the ultimate "Big Brother" tool. His inaugural address over the new system explains:

*170  Fontana: A Pocket History of Appalachia*

It is fitting, therefore, on this 168th anniversary of the Declaration of Independence, that Fontana Dam should institute an activity which is an important advancement in the construction industry.

Today at Fontana Dam we inaugurate and use for the first time on a major construction project anywhere in the world, an outdoor public address system for use in connection with the job we are here to do.

The Fontana Public Address System is but another step in the program of this project and of the Tennessee Valley Authority to nurture the atmosphere of contentment, satisfaction and happiness within and among the men and women who are doing this important and essential wartime work.

The system goes into operation on a continuous basis on all shifts today, Independence Day, July 4, 1944. It will reproduce music for your enjoyment while working and during your off duty hours. It will give you important war news almost as quickly as the news is made. It will tell you things of job interest—what the plans of work are to be, and so forth. It will be used to keep you abreast with the things being done to

### Plan of construction plant (map on opposite page).

INDEX—AGGREGATE & CONCRETE HANDLING PLANT:

| | | | |
|---|---|---|---|
| A | QUARRY | 5 | WAREHOUSE |
| B | PRIMARY CRUSHER | 6 | MACHINE & ELECTRICAL SHOP & GARAGE |
| C | PRIMARY STOCK PILE | 7 | CONCRETE TESTING LABORATORY |
| D | STANDARD CONE CRUSHER BUILDING | 8 | DRILL SHOP |
| E | SHORT HEAD CONE CRUSHER BUILDING | 9 | FIELD ENGINEERS OFFICE |
| F | SCREENING STRUCTURE & SURGE BINS | 10 | RIGGERS HOUSE |
| G | ROD MILLS | 11 | SHOP AREA TOILET & LOCKERS |
| H | HYDROSEPARATOR & CLASSIFIER | 12 | DRINKING WATER COOLING HOUSE |
| J | AGGREGATE SIZING SCREEN STRUCTURE & STACKERS | 13 | TRANSPORTATION OFFICE |
| | | 14 | SAFETY ENGINEERS OFFICE |
| K | AGGREGATE STORAGE PILES | 15 | TIME OFFICE |
| L | RINSING SCREENS | 16 | DOWNSTREAM RIVER GAGE |
| M | MIXING PLANT | 18 | GASOLINE & OIL STORAGE |
| N | CEMENT SILOS | 19 | GASOLINE & OIL PUMP HOUSE |
| P | CONCRETE HOPPERS | 20 | CARPENTER SHOP |
| R | CEMENT UNLOADING POINT—3 ROBINSON TANKS & SHED | 21 | COMPRESSOR HOUSE |
| | | 22 | CEMENT SHED |
| S | WATER TANKS | 23 | DYNAMITE HOUSE |
| T | RAW WATER PUMPS | 24 | CAP HOUSE |
| U | WATER TANKS | 25 | NITRAMON HOUSE |
| V | REFRIGERATION PLANT | 26 | DRILL SHOP |
| W | RAW WATER INTAKE FOR COOLING WATER | 27 | PERSONNEL OFFICE |
| X | PIPE SHOP | 28 | TOILET |
| Y | AUXILIARY BATCHING & SAND RECLAIMING PLANT | 29 | CHANGE HOUSE |
| | | 30 | FIELD SUPERINTENDENT & MASTER MECHANIC |
| Z | AUXILIARY CEMENT UNLOADING PLANT | 31 | SHEET METAL SHOP |
| AA | CEMENT UNLOADING POINT—ONE ROBINSON TANK & SHED (END OF JOB) | 32 | MEDICAL EXAMINATION BUILDING |
| | | 33 | QUARRY TRUCK REPAIR SHOP |
| | | 34 | DYNAMITE HOUSE |
| | | 35 | OBSERVATION PLATFORM |
| | | 36 | TOOL HOUSE |
| INDEX—BUILDINGS: | | 37 | CARPENTRY OFFICE & PLATFORM |
| | | 38 | GENERAL FOREMANS OFFICE |
| 1 | SUBSTATION NO.2 | 39 | PAINT SHOP |
| 2 | FILTER PLANT | 40 | QUARRY OFFICE |
| 3 | ADMINISTRATION BUILDING | 41 | SPILLWAY OFFICE |
| 4 | PRIMARY SUBSTATION & SUBSTATION NO.1 | 42 | REINFORCING STEEL OFFICE |

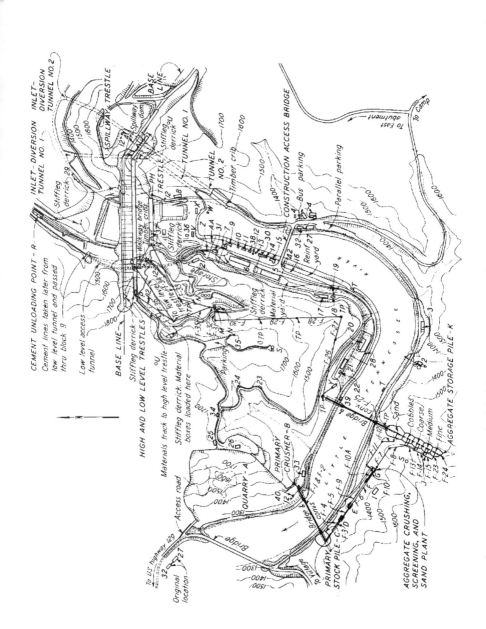

TVA

**Looking downstream through damsite, coffer dam in foreground.**

prevent accidents and how you can best work safely. It will give you information as to the progress of War Bond purchases. It will announce the various events as they are scheduled—such things as Union Meetings and meetings of other kinds. It will advise you of the activities of your Labor-Management Committee, your Transportation Committees and the various other groups which have and are continuously working to improve the working and living conditions at Fontana. The system will be used to give you the facts on all situations which develop from time to time. It will no longer be necessary to pay any attention to the rumors which usually pass from mouth to mouth on all manner of subjects—because 99 and nine-tenths of those are usually wrong anyway. Now you will be given the exact facts and you can then judge for yourself.

The music feature will be of real importance and it is hoped that you will enjoy it…

Some listeners reported that the music was played at a slightly faster speed than normal in hopes that workers trying to keep up with the tempo would work faster. Many workers worked seven days per week, sometimes for more than a year without a day off.

Wages ranged from $.50/hour for a beginning apprentice to $1.88 per hour for a skilled trades foreman, which was very good for the time. Almost always the work was dirty and physically demanding and quite often dangerous.

Since much land acquisition and preliminary engineering for the dam had been done by Alcoa, the first engineers and crews of the Construction and Maintenance Division were able to start work as soon as the project was authorized. In fact, a few TVA crews had been doing preparatory work on the site several months before the official January 1, 1942, starting date. After rudimentary accommodations and construction facilities were set up, the first order of business was to reroute the river. Easy to say, more complicated to do.

On March 20, 1942, two diversion tunnels were initiated on the east or Graham County side of the dam site. A plethora of work on support facilities and actual dam construction were carried out simultaneously throughout the project. Just 90 days later, the first 37 foot diameter tunnel was holed through. By September 6, 1942, coffer dams had been completed on either side of the dam site

**High trestle above base of dam.**

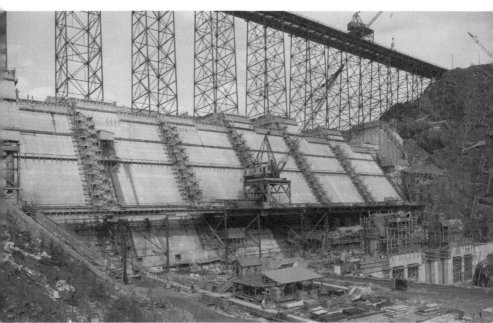

TVA

**Primary blast at the rock quarry.**

and the river was routed through the diversion tunnels. A few weeks later a railroad tunnel was completed through the west or Swain County abutment of the dam. This allowed rail transport of materials from the existing railroad that ran down the river upstream of the dam to the extensive construction shops located just downstream from the dam site. The tunnel would later be fitted with an 84-inch Howell-Bunger valve to create a very rare low level drain for the lake.

The primary material in Fontana Dam is concrete. Over 2,813,000 cubic yards were needed to complete the 480 foot high, 2,662 foot long structure. That equals well over 300,000 modern concrete truck loads. This concrete was manufactured and placed in an incredibly short period of time. In fact, the world's record for placing concrete was set on July 3, 1944, when 10,755 cubic yards was placed in one 24 hour period. I do not believe this record will ever be broken because people today will simply not work that hard, that fast, for so long. "They didn't beg you to do it, they just told you to do it or go home, whichever you wanted to do," concrete worker Bob Vickers remembered. "We worked Saturday and Sunday and all, twenty four hours a day. The only time we would stop is if something would break down, and then, by God, everybody went to fix it."

Concrete is made from cement, water, gravel, and sand. The cement was shipped in by rail and unloaded on the upstream side of the dam. It was then blown through pipes with compressed air to the silos at the mixing plant. The water was pumped from the river. The gravel and sand, by far the largest volume aggregate, was manufactured on site. A large rock quarry was developed about one mile downstream from the dam site on the Swain County side of the river. After the overburden was removed, blasting holes were drilled into the solid rock face of the mountain. These holes were loaded with DuPont's explosive Nitramon-A and detonated to bring down large quantities of rock. The largest single blast used 104 tons of Nitramon and brought down over 600,000 tons of rock. Even though the quarry blasts could certainly be heard and often felt in the village, mountain ridges between the two dampened the effect. One night Jimmy Marsh and a few other Dam Kids decided to take the Barton boys' red bone hound, Drum, up on the mountain for a hunt. They had gotten pretty high up the mountain and had just released the hound to begin the hunt, when all of a sudden the woods turned bright red. A moment later the trees started trembling, then came the loudest boom the group had ever heard. When the boys regained their composure

**Rock conveyors from aggregate storage to the mixing plant.**

and realized it had been a big shot in the quarry and their position on the mountain was not shielded from the effect, they started to look for Drum. But the big hound was no where to be found, so they gave up on the hunt and headed back to the village. Upon arriving at the Barton's house, they found old Drum sitting on the front porch—some said the dog was grinning.

**Concrete mixing plant.**

The blasted quarry rock was loaded with large electric shovels into diesel dump trucks and transported to the primary crusher. Since level land for all the construction shops and facilities below the dam site was extremely limited, an ingenious system of conveyors, some suspended across the river, was constructed to move the rock and sand toward its destination in the dam. From the primary crusher it went across the river to the secondary crushers, then to the screening plant in an adjacent valley where the various sizes of rock and sand were separated and stockpiled. In the bottom of the little valley where the stockpiles were located, a conveyor inside a heavy wooden tunnel had been constructed. Doors or vents in the roof of the tunnel could be remotely opened. This allowed the appropriate size and amount of material to fall onto the conveyor and continue its journey back across the river to the concrete mixing plant.

High above most of the hubbub of the construction plant in the river valley floor worked the cement-dust covered concrete mixer operators, who were possibly the most important men on the job. The work moved so fast that if their work was not to specification it would be buried before the khaki-clad concrete quality engineers could discover the error. The plant was located high enough on the west or Swain County side of the dam site that it could be used throughout the project. The aggregates were delivered and batched to be placed into "five Smith mixers which were of 4-cubic-yard capacity, size 112-5, tilting type, front-end charge, equipped with pneumatic tilt and tilt control valve, automatic pneumatic tilting frame lock, and each driven by a 75-horsepower, 440 volt, 3 phase, 60 cycle, ball bearing, splash-proof, squirrel-cage, high-starting-torque, low-starting-current, electric motor." Whew!

The mixed concrete then went on the next ingenious part of its ride. By now, the progress of thousands of men depended on the timely and accurate delivery of the mixers' product. The concrete traveled by conveyor from the mixing plant to wet batch hoppers that were placed at the end of trestles or bridges which spanned the dam site. Two trains consisting of a heavy duty flatcar pulled by a dinkey locomotive ran on each trestle. Each flatcar carried four large concrete buckets and space for a fifth. As one train was being unloaded out on the trestle, the other was being loaded under the wet batch hoppers. When loaded, the train

**Khaki clad inspector and a concerned worker.**

TVA

pulled out on the trestle just in time for the overhead cranes to place the last empty bucket from the other train in the vacant space and pick up a full bucket. As soon as the last full bucket was picked up, the train returned to the hopper for another load. Several pours would be going on simultaneously on the dam below and the entire affair was orchestrated so that the movement of concrete buckets was continuous. When the concrete was placed in the reusable forms, workers with mechanical vibrators would compact the mass into its final position.

The work was dangerous. Stories of workers being buried in the dam have been popular. But the reality was that it would have been more trouble and time consuming to finish the concrete around the body than it was to remove it and continue pouring. Anyway, the void created by a decayed body would not pass the specifications of the concrete inspectors. Probably a few fingers did find their final resting place in the mass of concrete. Even though worker safety was a major concern, the nature and speed

**Spillway tube construction was referred to as tedious.**

of the work led to accidents. John Lee Patterson, former Raburn County, Georgia Superintendent and Mayor of Clayton related to his grandson David Lee Payne for the excellent publication *Foxfire* that one worker almost did become part of the dam:

> There was this fellow in there working and he didn't hear the foreman tell him to get out. 'Course there was a lot of racket with the steel work going on and the crane turning. He was working in there facing toward the form, and when the concrete hit him, it slapped him up against the inside of the form. It didn't kill him right then, but when they stripped the form there he stood, set up in the concrete. They never could trace him down to where he was until they stripped the form, and there he was a'standing there with a hoe in his hand, and they just slipped him out. When concrete dries, it shrinks up, and when they lifted the form, there he was.

On another occasion Mr. Patterson saw:

> …a gas shovel fall over that mountain, and it went 300 feet down that mountain turning over like a car, and it didn't even kill the fellow. I think it just broke one of the bones in his arm just above the wrist. He stayed in the cab of that thing all the way down that mountain. It looked like a beer can mashed up when they started salvaging it. I mean it tore that thing all to pieces. That was one more job.

I think that Mr. Patterson may also believe in the old adage "tis a poor piece of cloth that stand no embroidery." The official record states that during the construction, 14 people were killed, 11 people suffered permanent injuries, and 447 had temporary injuries.

Even though concrete placement on the top portion of the dam continued until April 3, 1945, the diversion tunnels were closed on November 7, 1944, and the reservoir began filling. The first power generated at the new dam went on line on January 20, 1945, only $36\frac{1}{2}$ months after construction had begun, about half the time normally required to complete such a massive project during wartime. At the beginning of the 21st century, probably 10 to 15 years would be required to complete a project of similar size and scope.

## Chapter 12
# The Change Back

Reservoir preparation was the part of the project that effected area residents the most. In fact, the area would be almost completely depopulated. The first contact for many residents was with TVA surveyors and map makers. Over 20 different types of surveys were done on the project area. First, existing topographic maps and new aerial photographs were examined to establish the approximate parameters of the project area. Field surveys were then undertaken for each specific purpose. A total of 79,947 acres of land were eventually surveyed and mapped.

Prior to 1941, Alcoa had purchased just over 15,000 acres, including the dam site and much of the land that would be covered by the lake. This land was transferred to TVA under the Fontana Agreement in late 1941, allowing for the immediate start-up when the project was funded on December 17, 1941. The priority for land acquisition was to purchase the rest of the land that would be covered by water so that reservoir preparation could be completed. Field investigations were conducted to determine the extent to which individual farm tracts would be affected. Land acquisition maps were made that showed the land owner and tract size, as well as landscape features such as streams, pastures, roads, and trails—and all improvements, even the corn cribs and the outhouses.

*The Fontana Project,* TVA's official report on the project states "TVA's governing price policy is to purchase land and rights required at prices which will enable owners to relocate or re-establish themselves on properties at least equal in value to those they previously owned." The appraisal staff studied various factors such as land use, previous sales, and trends in the real estate market to establish price ranges for the various land classifications and improvements. The bottom line was that "Prices to be paid for the land were fixed by TVA's appraisal staff. No price trading was permitted to enter into the negotiations and the property was either purchased at the appraised price or condemned." The average price paid for the 68,291.97 acres that were eventually purchased was $37.76 per acre. This was one of the lowest prices paid for reservoir lands in TVA history and "reflects the mountainous character and remoteness of the reservoir setting." The "war effect" approach was commonly used in the negotiations for purchase of the 1,064 tracts secured for the project. Not counting the Alcoa lands, 88.4 % of the land owners sold voluntarily at the appraised price, 8.2 % by condemnation in order to clear up title problems, and only 3.4 % by condemnation because the owners refused to sell. Property owners were not required to surrender their property until it was actually needed for the project. Other than in the dam construction area, most residents stayed on until mid-1944—many worked at the dam or the copper mine and were encouraged to stay.

*Calhoun bottom and island on the Little Tennessee before the flood.*

*The Fontana Project* states that "Reservoir clearance is rated as one of the most hazardous of all logging operations. Unquestionably, the terrain in this reservoir was more mountainous, rugged, and inaccessible than any of the TVA's other projects." Dam construction supervisors often complained about the abilities and independent attitudes of the local labor force, but the reservoir clearing bosses thought the local boys were splendid. Generations of logging and mountainside farming experience produced highly trained woods workers. Most Americans knew the four points of the compass—north, south, east, and west. Many locals had adopted from their Indian neighbors three additional points—above, below, and here. About 500 workers, including a crew of

*The Change Back* **183**

TVA

***Cliffside reservoir clearing, workers suspended in safety harness.***

about 50 Cherokee Indians, sometimes suspended in safety saddles, cut trees that often landed several hundred feet below.

The entire reservoir was not cleared. Trees and vegetation whose tops did not protrude above the maximum drawdown elevation of 1,540 feet were left standing. This not only saved labor but also provides a sort of sieve to catch the inevitable silt washed into the lake, resulting in cleaner water. Above this a 2,151 acre strip was cut and wired down in place. From elevation 1,540 to 1,710, all vegetation was cut, piled, and burned. About three million board feet of lumber was salvaged and sawed by private contractor for use in dam and village construction.

Roads, railroads, utility lines, and cemeteries were both abandoned and relocated. Even part of a river was moved. Just over 28 miles of new highway was built to reconnect existing roads that were interrupted by the reservoir construction. Most of these new roads were in the area between Bryson City and the Stecoah community.

The Carolina and Tennessee Southern Railroad from Bushnell to the town of Fontana was completely inundated. And since everything the line served was also drowned, it was abandoned and removed. Twenty-four miles of the Murphy Branch of the Southern

TVA

***Southern Railway's Murphy Branch relocation at the Almond Trestle.***

Railroad between Bryson City and Wesser, North Carolina was also submerged. Because this line still served the towns of Andrews and Murphy, it was rebuilt outside the reservoir area. The tracks from Wesser along the Nantahala River to the high trestle at Almond were benched in higher on the mountain to avoid the new lake. From the Almond trestle to Bryson City a completely new route was taken across country. The reroute is eight miles shorter than the original route along the rivers and is still operated today by the Great Smoky Mountain Railway.

New steel for bridge construction was not available due to wartime restrictions. Structural steel was salvaged from bridge removal on other TVA projects to build the railroad bridges over the Tuckassegee River at Bryson City and the 777 foot long, 160 foot high trestle bridge at Almond. TVA engineers soon realized the salvaged steel was not sufficient to complete the bridges, so they came up with a solution that was indicative of dealing with material shortages throughout the project. They didn't have much steel but they had plenty of dynamite. Two steel girder railroad bridges crossed the Nantahala River at Wesser where the river made a sharp horseshoe curve. The engineers blasted a new river channel through solid rock, eliminating the horseshoe and the need for the two bridges. This freed up 600 feet of deck plate girders to complete the other bridges. The new river channel, today known as Big Wesser Falls, is located just downstream from the Nantahala Outdoor Center. The old horseshoe curve in the river is now just a placid pond.

The TVA technical report *Surveying, Mapping, and Related Engineering* states:

> The removal of graves from areas to be inundated by the impoundage of TVA reservoirs is a comparatively minor construction feature, but there is not a more important phase of the over-all project construction schedule from the point of view of residents of the vicinity. Deeply rooted sentiments, traditions, and customs which attach to the graves of the dead demand scrupulous care in dealing with relatives, moving graves, and keeping accurate records on every affected grave.
>
> Since the beginning of the first reservoir project, the removal of graves from the areas to be flooded has been looked upon as a regrettable necessity and deference to the wishes of the relatives has been, as far as it was possible to make it so, a prime consideration. State laws and regulations applying to the disinterment, transportation, and reinterment of bodies and remains have been observed meticulously and every effort has been made to conduct all removal operations in a respectful manner.

Graves that would be inundated or rendered inaccessible by flooding of existing roads were subject to removal. Relatives, if they could be found, were given three choices: leave the grave undisturbed even if it would be underwater; move the remains to a re-internment cemetery at TVA expense; or move the remains to a distant cemetery, with long distance transportation costs paid by the family. Most graves in cemeteries that were not to be flooded were left undisturbed. Some graves that would be submerged were moved. And some were left to rest underneath the water of the new lake.

During a major drawdown of Fontana Lake in 1990, I was exploring the old town of Judson with TVA archeologist Danny Olinger. We were trying to orient ourselves by referring to the detailed land acquisition map. Although many features such as chimney bases, stone walls, and even the preserved stumps of hedge rows were evident, we could not quite figure out the scene. Then we stumbled on a gravestone inscribed "Louise, Daughter of C.C. and Pearl Ashe, Born Dead Feb. 13, 1811." Suddenly, we knew exactly where we were. It was sort of surreal, that a monument of the dead, in a dead town, had helped us orient ourselves.

*"Louise, Daughter of C.C. and Pearl Ashe, Born Dead Feb. 13, 1811."*

References have been made to the facts that almost 80,000 acres were surveyed and mapped, and over 68,000 acres of land were acquired for the Fontana Project—yet only 10,670 acres were actually covered with water. When the Great Smoky Mountains National Park was first established in 1934, most park promoters envisioned that the new park would encompass all the land from the state line ridge down to the Little Tennessee and Tuckassegee Rivers. Due to the presence of a half dozen small towns, several copper mines, railroads, and the potential for water power development, coupled with a lack of funds, a strip of about 46,000 acres just north of the rivers was excluded from the original park boundary.

This area was served by North Carolina State Highway 288. Knowing of Alcoa's land purchases and plans to build a 200-foot high dam at the Fontana site, the Forney Creek Road District of Swain County floated two bond issues totaling $700,000 to finance the construction of Highway 288 in 1926, to replace the old Joseph Welch river turnpike and the Carolina and Tennessee Southern Railroad that would be flooded by Alcoa's reservoir. Highway 288 connected Bryson City and U.S. Highway 129 at Deals Gap. Even though it provided access to Tennessee and beyond, the winding, mountainside, unpaved road was mostly used by local traffic. The first TVA personnel who arrived at Fontana via this road decided a new access road from Deals Gap would be the first order of business. U.S. Highway 129 from Deals Gap toward

Tennessee had 318 curves in 11 miles, but at least it was paved.

It was soon realized that a substantial portion of Highway 288 between Fontana and Bryson City would be flooded by the reservoir behind TVA's 480-foot high dam, thus cutting off access to the families that lived in the region. The estimate to relocate the highway using comparable low grade construction standards was $1,200,000, a figure TVA deemed more than the value of the land served. Furthermore, the War Production Board had indicated that reconstruction of the road was not of sufficient importance to justify the expenditure of materials and manpower required for the work during the war. TVA proposed an alternate solution that would "cost only $1,075,000 and would result in advantages to the mutual benefit of all concerned."

Extensive negotiations between TVA, the state of North Carolina, Swain County, and U.S. Department of Interior on behalf of the National Park Service led to the quadrilateral 1943 AGREE-

**Wilson Span Bridge over Hazel Creek, replaced in the late 1980's.**

HOLLAND COLLECTION

MENT. In 1940, through a general refunding program, Swain County assumed from the Forney Creek road district the then $700,000 (including interest) road bond debt. And the North Carolina State Highway and Public Works Commission took over the maintenance of Highway 288. The 1943 Agreement had the following provisions:

1) TVA would acquire by "purchase, right of eminent domain, or otherwise" all of the land, approximately 44,400 acres, between the existing park boundary and the north shore of the new reservoir, excluding 1,900 acres owned by the North Carolina Exploration Company containing the Fontana copper mine.

2) Immediately following its acquisition, TVA would transfer these lands to the Park Service for inclusion into the Great Smoky Mountains National Park.

3) The Park Service would build a park road through the newly acquired lands from a point near Fontana Dam to a point near Bryson City as soon as construction funds were appropriated by Congress after the war.

4) The state of North Carolina would build a road from Bryson City to a point designated by the Park Service to connect the new park road to U.S. Highway 19. The state would also take over the maintenance of the TVA built access road from Deals Gap to Fontana Dam.

5) The state would pay TVA $100,000 to help purchase the land.

6) TVA would pay the North Carolina Local Government Commission $400,000 to set up a trust fund for Swain County to be used exclusively to pay off the principle of the outstanding road bond on Highway 288 which would become due on August 1, 1975.

Except for the road construction, all parties had fulfilled their obligations under the agreement by late 1944. Highway 288 also provided access for a number of scattered settlements, primarily Cable Cove, located on the south side of the river whose residents either crossed the river by boat or climbed steep trails over the surrounding mountains to the outside world. In addition to the 44,000 acres on the north side of the reservoir, 4,500 acres on the south side were also acquired. This land was transferred to the U.S.

Forest Service.

The original date of December 31, 1943, for surrendering possession of lands acquired by TVA was eventually extended to November 1, 1944. Some affected families had left the area earlier in the project period, but many residents worked on the dam or in the copper mines and were encouraged to stay as long as possible. About a month before closure of the diversion tunnels on November 7, 1944, which began the filling of the reservoir, the mass exodus reached full speed.

Wartime shortages of building materials caused families to remove a large percentage of lumber and other materials from the old structures. Difficulties of access meant residents had to resort to many devices in moving. Sleds were used on sled roads and trails leading to the highway, and in some cases it was necessary for family members to hand carry their belongings to points where vehicles could be accessed. TVA, the Office of Defense Transportation, and the Office of Price Administration furnished trucks to help 1,311 evicted families move their personal belongings, household goods, crops, livestock, and salvaged building materials. Duane Oliver's father bought the town of Fontana from the mining company for $50. He dismantled the buildings, and shipped the lumber to Hazelwood, North Carolina by rail. Oliver now lives in a house that was partially constructed from these salvaged materials.

The buildings and debris left after the residents were gone was burned by TVA crews. On Struttin Street in Proctor on Hazel Creek the floor plan of one of the torched houses can still be made out—the cast iron cook stove fell to the ground where the kitchen was and a metal bed frame marks a bedroom. Oliver remembered "standing on the graveyard hill in Possum Hollow and watching the Franklin Store and Warehouse being put to the torch by the TVA. We children found this exciting, not realizing that a town and a way of life were dying."

The reservoir drowned the villages of Fontana, the Fontana mine camp, Ritter, Wayside, Dorsey, Marcus, Bushnell, Japan, Forney, Judson, and Almond. Major drawdowns of the lake reveal foundations, stone walls, grave markers, and other structures that would not burn, creating an eerie museum of the past. If you go visit, remember that all the remains are federally protected artifacts and definitely should not be disturbed. When the war broke out, the residents of the village of Japan (pronounced "jay-pan" after a local clover) talked of changing the name of their settlement, but upon learning of TVA's plans, they just let it die as Japan. Newspapers of the day ran headlines that read "TVA to drown Japan."

Many displaced residents relocated in western North Carolina or east Tennessee. Most of these people cooperated with the removal—they were very patriotic, and were doing their part for the war effort. Former resident, Gay Calhoun recalled his feelings about leaving while visiting his boyhood home at the Fontana Copper Mine camp during the lake drawdown in 1990. "When I went out of here, it didn't bother me," he said. "It must have been a terrible change for me, because I had grown up here to 17 years old and had never been much of anywhere except Maryville and Knoxville a time or two. But I went out of here and went to Orlando, Florida in the service to get my training, and never did miss this place, never did miss nobody."

Some family members who had been overseas in the Armed Forces during the exodus could not immediately find their families upon their return. A few did not even know about the addition of the north shore lands to the Fontana Project until they returned to

**Bushnell hotel and store.**

OLIVER COLLECTION

**Village of Japan.**

find their home and family gone. After the war, most folks settled into their new lives in their new homeplaces and did not look back—at least at first.

During the late 1940's and the 1950's, North Carolina Governor Luther Hodges and others lobbied extensively to precipitate the road construction promised in the 1943 Agreement. Conversely, as early as February 1953 a letter writing campaign to Park Service officials and members of Congress was undertaken by Edgar L. McDaniel, Jr., a frequent camper and hiker in the Fontana area to protest the construction of the North Shore Road. In 1959, the state of North Carolina fulfilled its obligation by completing 2.67 miles of road from Bryson City to the park boundary. Finally, between 1963 and 1971, the Park Service constructed six miles of the long awaited North Shore Road from the Bryson City end, terminating at a 1,200-foot long tunnel. This section of road, officially named Lakeshore Drive, has been locally dubbed "The Road To Nowhere."

Construction of the road exposed rock containing pyrite minerals known as the Anakeesta Formation. When the pyrites are exposed to air and water they produce a sulfuric acid runoff. The

*Gay Calhoun.*

runoff reached nearby streams causing fish kills. This effect can be combated with modern engineering techniques that encapsulate the sulfide bearing rock—but this adds considerable expense to the road construction process.

Environmental damage gave those opposed to the road leverage. A briefing statement issued by the Great Smoky Mountains National Park in 1980 states "During construction, it became apparent that severe damage was being done within the park. The further construction progressed, the larger road cuts and fills and scars were becoming. As a result, the Service stopped construction after completing work on a tunnel seven miles from the boundary and ceased requesting congressional appropriations."

Meanwhile, the future of the North Shore Road and, in fact, the Carolina side of the park became a political football. The following chronological summary of events was prepared by Bryson City author and historian George Ellison:

**1965**—*Amendment proposed to 1943 agreement substituting a 34.7 mile trans-mountain road to Townsend, Tennessee from Bryson City as an alternative to the North Shore road. Swain County and North Carolina agreed. Secretary of Interior ultimately refused to build the road (December 10, 1967) but promised to build recreational facilities and a marina. They were never built.*

***1968***—*Governor Dan Moore of North Carolina proposed an extension of the Blue Ridge Parkway to Deep Creek (Bryson City) as an alternative to the other two roads.*

***1969***—*Secretary of Interior Hickel instructed the director of the National Park Service to prepare a report on the settlement problem and to propose solutions.*

***1971***—*National Park Service issued proposed solutions to the controversy in its* Transportation Concepts: Great Smoky Mountains. *Proposals included a system of roadways encircling the Park, a Visitor Transit Concept, a Foothills Parkway extension, and others.*

***1971-1974***—*Various congressional attempts were made by Congressman Roy Taylor and others to resolve the problem. No resolution.*

On September 3, 1964 Congress passed the Wilderness Act that would, among other things, prohibit the use of mechanized equipment on land designated as Wilderness areas. The designation precluded activities such as logging and road building and was primarily assigned to roadless national forest lands. Ellison's chronological summary continues:

***July 1974***—*Park superintendent Vincent Ellis proposed 76% of the Park be designated Wilderness. Proposal opposed by various groups unless linked with settlement of 1943 dispute.*

***1975***—*Meeting held between NC Department of Natural Resources, NPS, TVA, Swain County, and environmental groups to discuss settlement. First discussion of cash settlement. '10 Point Proposal' put forward.*

***1976-1977***—*Proposals and debate continued. No resolution.*

In the mid 1970's, Helen Cable Vance, valedictorian of the last graduating class at Proctor High School on Hazel Creek in 1943, along with her sister Mildred Cable Johnson and other former residents, organized the North Shore Cemetery Association. Later renamed the Fontana North Shore Historical Association, the group lobbied, and continues to do so, for the completion of the promised road. They held the first Proctor Cemetery decoration in 31 years on Sunday, July 30, 1978.

A southern mountain tradition, decoration day is an annual visit to place flowers on the graves and remember deceased family members. By the early 1980's, a regular schedule of decorations was held each year for as many of the 26 North Shore cemeteries as could be found. Getting to most of the cemeteries is quite an adventure. Descendants gather at boat ramps on the south shore of the lake to board passenger boats contracted from Fontana Village by the Park Service for the first leg of the journey across the lake. Upon reaching the North Shore, they board Park Service trucks and jeeps, also brought over by barge, to travel the old roads that were cut off from the rest of the world with the impoundment of the lake. The last leg of each trip is made on foot since most cemeteries were located on top of ridges. A few cemeteries never had nearby roads and must be accessed completely on foot. Once everyone finally arrives, flowers are placed on the graves and hymns are sung, followed by preaching and prayers. After the service the group retires to a communal meal hauled over in coolers, packs, and picnic baskets. For many years I drove one of the passenger boats and had the distinct pleasure of attending dozens of decorations, although I sometimes worried about the safety of the older and more frail participants.

Many former residents feel that their government lied to them. They were told that their families' land was needed for the war effort and almost all cooperated. Many were also told that the North Shore road would provide reasonable access to their cemeteries. I do not think anyone challenges the fact that a promise for a road was made—it is clearly stated in the 1943 Agreement. Conversely, the 1943 Agreement does not mention cemeteries or access thereto. The 1980 Park Service briefing statement reads "The association pressed for completion of the road. They see it as a means of easy access to the cemeteries which is not the case. Even if the road were built, it would not go near many of the old cemeteries."

The legal and moral aspects of the controversy will probably never be completely resolved to everyone's satisfaction but one thing is for sure—the North Shore road will be an emotional issue for former residents and their descendants for many years to come.

Ellison's chronological summary continues:

**August 1978**—*Interior Secretary Cecil Andrus visited Swain County to 'listen and learn'.*

**October 1978**—*Secretary Andrus proposes six member study committee to meet in Waynesville, North Carolina.*

**Jan. 15, 1979**—*Fontana Agreement Committee met in Waynesville chaired by David Felmet. 'Twelve Point Proposal' formulated, including a cash settlement in 'excess of 10 million dollars'.*

**Nov. 28, 1980**—*Secretary of Interior Andrus finally agrees to 'value' of proposed cash settlement at 1.3 million dollars compounded annually from 1940 (In 1980 the total amount was $9,609,582. the current total as of June 1991 is $16,044,321.43). This decision and settlement figure is set forth in the Briefing Statement and Decision Sheet dated November 28, 1980.*

**1980**—*HR 8419 introduced by Congressman Lamar Gudger provided for a 9.5 million cash settlement and cancellation of 3.2 million dollar FHA school construction loan to Swain County. House Bill passed. Congress adjourned prior to Senate passage (lame duck).*

**1982**—*Congressman Jamie Clarke makes various attempts to resolve controversy.*

**July 14, 1983**—*Congressman Clarke introduces HR 3567 which provides for cash settlement to Swain County of 9.5 million, along with forgiveness of FHA indebtedness.*

**Oct. 7, 1983**—*Senators Sasser and Baker (Tenn.) introduce S1947 establishing 467,000 acres of GSMNP as Wilderness. Bill includes 9.5 million dollar settlement for Swain County and forgiveness of FHA indebtedness (HR 4267 introduced in House-identical bill).*

**Nov. 14, 1983**—*Senate Bill 2813 introduced by Senator Jesse Helms. Establishes wilderness of 400,000 acres, excluding 44,000 acres north of Fontana Lake. Includes $950,000 to provide primitive road access to cemeteries. Also includes 9.5 million cash settlement to Swain County and forgiveness of FHA indebtedness. Senate hearings are held in Bryson City and Washington. None of the 1983 legislation was enacted.*

**Feb. 13, 1989**—*Chairman of Great Smoky Mountain Park Commission (Neil Murphy) writes Senator Sanford that the Commission favors indemnifying Swain County. The Commission opposes a North Shore road* *and linkage to the Wilderness issue. The Commission favors formalized guarantee of cemetery access.*

**Feb. 18, 1991**—*Swain County Commissioners request Congressman Taylor and Senators Sanford and Helms to assist in finally bringing the 1943 Agreement controversy to closure.*

News Flash! Less than two weeks before the November 2000 elections, U.S. Rep. Charles Taylor and U.S. Sen. Jesse Helms won approval for $16 million toward the construction of the North Shore Road. The money was contained in a transportation appropriations bill signed by President Bill Clinton. Swain County administrator Linda Cable's reaction to the news was "It's certainly a surprise, this is the first time this has crossed my desk."

The Great Smoky Mountains National Park administration was equally unprepared. "This is a complete surprise to us. We certainly didn't request this funding. The Park Service has taken the position since 1980 that the road should not be built," said Smokies spokesman, Bob Miller. The last estimate of the project's cost was $136 million. Ron Leatherwood, North Carolina Board of Transportation member, said most of the $16 million would probably go toward extensive environmental work. Sam Neill, Rep. Taylor's opponent in the election said of the surprise funding "This is nothing more than an election year fraud." The pot continues to be stirred.

The dispute between W.S. Adams and George Westfeldt over the ownership of the copper strike on the Sugar Fork of Hazel Creek became the longest court case in the history of the United States—26 years. Now the North Shore section of the Fontana area, without even any people living there, can claim another record that will also probably never be broken, the longest unresolved issue debated by the United States Congress—55 years and counting.

Chapter 13

# The Village of Many Lives

An almost unbelievable quiet fell over the Fontana area in 1946. The sounds of loggers, miners, railroads, dam builders, families going about their daily lives, and even the sound of the river itself were all gone. An old lady had told the TVA land buyer who came to purchase her property "That dam is going to be the ruination of this here country."

Others had a different view of the future. A front page article in the August 5, 1943, edition of the *Bryson City Times* proclaimed:

> Under the agreement signed last week by Swain County, State of North Carolina, and the Tennessee Valley Authority, Swain County will be paid in trust $400,000 to be applied on outstanding bond indebtedness, the landowners will be paid for their property and the Smoky Mountains National Park will be increased by some 44,000 acres of land. If these were the only factors to be considered in the transaction it would appear that Swain County came out on the losing end of the deal. But happily, this isn't the case. The potentialities for the greatest era of development and progress for Bryson City and vicinity are also written in the agreement.
>
> The National Park Service says that as soon as money is made available after the war it will build a modern highway along the shores of Fontana Lake connecting Bryson City with the TVA access highway at Fontana Dam, making it a through highway to Deal's Gap 50 miles west of here. Anyone with the smallest amount of imagination can visualize

what a road of this kind will mean to Bryson City. The State Highway Commission has said, definitely, that it will build the same type of road from Bryson City to connect the Park road. Park Service officials have not made public any plans for recreational development along Fontana Lake and this new scenic highway, but we do know that they have rather ambitious plans in mind.

When this highway is built by the Park Service, the developments inaugurated, and we feel confidently they will be soon after the war, then there is nothing that can keep Bryson City from becoming the tourist center of Eastern America, unless it is possibly we who live here. There is great danger in the fact that we will not awaken to our opportunities, grasp them with a firm determination to make something of them and then go ahead and make Bryson City just as great as the future developments indicate that she should be.

Twenty years earlier Horace Kephart had heralded similar prosperity with the establishment of the Great Smoky Mountains National Park:

*If the Smokies are taken over for a park, immediately the construction of Federal highways and bridle-paths will begin, giving employment at fair wages to hundreds of mountaineers who are now eking out a scanty subsistence. Camp sites on the grand scale must at once be provided, with dining halls seating a thousand people or more, amusement halls, rest rooms, cottages for campers, and everything else that the millions would require.*

*Probably no hotels would be permitted in the park itself, but they would spring up like magic along the boundary line. A car of tourists, starting from one of these hotels in the morning, could spend the day running up one of the transmontane roads, following the sky-line road to another, and return to a hotel on the border for comfortable quarters at night.*

*Every trade and business associated with tourist life would plant itself on that park border and thrive. Real estate values would double, quadruple, multiply indefinitely. The mountain counties of far Western North Carolina would emerge from obscurity and become gems in the old State's crown.*

Both prognostications related roads to a tourist bonanza. In January of 2000, I conducted an informal survey of Swain County leaders asking why they thought Gatlinburg, Tennessee had experienced phenomenal tourist growth while Bryson City had not. Roads was the unanimous answer. Many respondents cited the North Shore Road as the missing link to prosperity. Others believed that a lack of good roads into the region was the culprit. From the time of the creation of the park, Gatlinburg was only a short drive from the city of Knoxville with its rail, bus, and highway connections to the rest of the country. Interestingly, most folks also added that the lack of tourist glut is what makes the Carolina side a more attractive place to live. Therefore, the lack of good roads can be viewed both as the bane and the savior of far western North Carolina.

Of course, tourism did become an important part of the region's economy, just not an overwhelming one. Considerable development occurred in Cherokee, North Carolina at the eastern end of the park's transmountain highway and scattered motels and tourist courts sprang up around the region. By the mid-1980's, Bryson City started experiencing a kind of slow motion tourist boom spurred by the development of whitewater sports on the nearby Nantahala River, and the creation of the Great Smoky Mountain Railway providing rail excursions on a portion of the Murphy Branch Railroad.

Nowadays, when someone mentions outdoor adventure sports, most folks envision city-dwelling pilgrims escaping to the mountains in their kayak and mountain bike festooned sport utility vehicles loaded with a plethora of camping, hiking, rock climbing, fly fishing, and assorted other gear. And over the past twenty years as the popularity of these "new" outdoor activities has exploded, western North Carolina has become the destination of choice. Places like the Nantahala, Tsali, and Looking Glass Rock have become world famous. But the idea of western North Carolina and other parts of the southern Appalachians being a mecca for outdoor sports is certainly not new.

In the late 1800's, George Vanderbilt chose western North Carolina to create the vast outdoor playground he called Biltmore Estate, part of which would later become the nucleus of Pisgah National Forest. His guests would spend glorious days cavorting in the back country engaged in the "new" pastimes of camping, hiking, and fishing.

Horace Kephart, a burnt-out librarian who longed for outdoor adventure, got off the train in Dillsboro, North Carolina in 1904. Within a few months he had settled into a small cabin on the Little Fork of the Sugar Fork of Hazel Creek at the abandoned Adams-Westfeldt copper mine in the Smokies. From this base camp, Kephart set about the business of outdoor adventure. He supported himself by writing articles about the outdoor skills he was honing in the popular outdoor magazines of the day; *Sports Afield, Outing Magazine, Field and Stream,* and others. By 1906 he had published *Camping and Woodcraft,* which is still highly valued today by outdoor enthusiasts in regard to basic techniques and timeless philosophy. And in 1913, he released *Our Southern Highlanders,* the classic study of southern Appalachian culture. Known as the Dean of American Campers, Kephart worked tirelessly toward the establishment of the Great Smoky Mountains National Park.

Kephart's writings helped transform the Hazel Creek/Fontana area from what he called "terra incognita" into a what's happening place to be for outdoor adventure. By the 1920's, many Americans had the time, money, and desire to recreate in the outdoors. To help satisfy the demand, J.G. Stikeleather established the Hazel Creek Fishing and Outing Club. For two decades, guests at the club reveled in the sublime pleasures of the outdoors. Other enthusiasts such as the Kress family, of department store fame, also built lodges in the area and joined in the fun. But in the early 1940's, World War II and the subsequent construction of Fontana Lake temporarily brought an end to the fun.

In the late 1940's the largest single tourist development in western North Carolina was the transformation of the almost deserted TVA construction village. Fontana Village was often referred to as "The Village of Five Lives" by Lucile K. Boyden, resort public relations director in the 1950's and 1960's. Mrs. Boyden was a prolific writer of promotional releases and advertisements. At management's request and with considerable editorial interference, she authored a booklet length advertisement for the property disguised as a history. Examination of old company files reveals that Mrs. Boyden tried hard to write an interesting historical narrative, but the bosses in Washington had their agenda. Yet, her basic premise survived the editorial onslaught and says much about the tenacity of the place.

The first Fontana, North Carolina was nothing more than a tent

*The Village of Many Lives* **203**

**The first Fontana, North Carolina—Monvale's lumber camp on Eagle Creek.**

camp set up in the spring of 1906 on the banks of Eagle Creek by Montvale Lumber Company. In addition to surveying their timber holdings, one of their first activities was to build a more substantial lumber town complete with homes, a commissary, the sawmill, and hotel. This second Fontana, located at the confluence of Eagle Creek and the Little Tennessee River, housed the same population, just at a slightly different location. All of the lumber towns had a post office, therefore a name for the place had to be chosen. The task fell to Mrs. George Leidy Wood, wife of the company vice-president. One story persists that the area was named after an Italian mineral prospector named Felice Fontaine who explored the southern mountains in the late 1700's. But Mrs. Wood later wrote:

*Shortly after we took up life in the pretty little tent-town, my husband suggested that we should give the place a name. Together, we searched through endless rail and postal guides for something suitable, but found nothing, mainly because the names all seemed too ordinary for a spot so beautiful. Finally, he asked that I coin a word for it. I thought of the lovely, flowering glens, the waterfalls that looked like fountains,*

**Monvale Lumber Co's hotel and commissary at the second Fontana.**

leaping from ledge to ledge, and eventually I worked out the word 'Fontana', a short word, musical, easy to spell.

    By 1927 Montvale Lumber Company's operations were winding down on Eagle Creek. On February 1, 1931, Montvale sold their Eagle Creek lands, including the little lumber town of Fontana, to the North Carolina Exploration Company, which had developed the nearby copper mine. This time the town stayed in the same place, but the population changed for its third life.

    Next, TVA brought big changes—the little town at the confluence of Eagle Creek and the Little T. would be drowned under hundreds of feet of water. A new town, at a new location, for a new population was built in Welch Cove and became the fourth reincarnation of the village called Fontana. From 1942 through 1945, with its 24 hour a day hustle and bustle, the new town was the second largest in western North Carolina. By late 1945, however, the big dam was complete and only a handful of TVA employees remained in the almost abandoned town. Throughout all this, two things remained constant—change and the post office.

TVA now had a complete town nestled deep in the Smoky Mountains—but was not sure just what to do with it. The Armed Services were approached to turn the place into a rest and recuperation facility to no avail. Meanwhile, a growing number of engineers and tourists were showing up to marvel at the giant dam. Realizing its location in the immediate vicinity of the Great Smoky Mountains National Park, the Nantahala National Forest, and the new lake, TVA advertised the availability of the village for lease as a recreational resort. In connection with engineering problems related to questions of highway access into the affected areas, TVA had begun studies of the recreational potentialities of Fontana Lake in 1942. But since all the land on the North Shore would be placed in the National Park and South Shore lands would be transferred to the U.S. Forest Service, TVA didn't actually do anything to provide for public recreation.

On April 24, 1946, Washington, D.C. based Government Services Inc. (G.S.I.) extended "the long arm of restoration and productivity into the Great Smoky Mountains of western North Carolina" by signing a long term lease with TVA and assumed operation of Fontana Village. Thus, the fifth life.

G.S.I., first called the Joint Welfare Association, was started during World War I to provide food service, recreation, and other needs for the large number of government employees who were brought into Washington. By 1926 the operation had grown considerably and was incorporated as a non-stock distributing corporation with Major General Ulysses S. Grant, III as chairman of the board. Originally operating hot dog stands on the mall, the

**Fontana Village and Dam, nestled deep in the Smokies.**

company became the primary food service provider in the federal buildings of Washington. Often mistakenly thought of as a government agency itself, the private company only did business with the federal government.

Evidently there was not much competition for the Fontana Village management lease. In a memo to Lucile Boyden, company president R.R. Ayers wrote:

> Also, I believe that it is not a true fact that TVA did not receive any bids. It has always been my understanding that they did receive bids or proposals from other concerns, but they were not satisfied with them inasmuch as no one wished to take on the responsibility of operation of the village on a year-round basis. This, of course, was one of the major requirements of TVA as they wished to be relieved of the responsibility and expense of maintaining the essential services; water plant, sewage disposal, electric lines, maintenance of the grounds, medical, feeding facilities, etc.

The first lease only included about half the village. Most of the permanent type houses were still occupied by TVA personnel, the school buildings were still in use, and the camp area had not been disassembled. The 1946 tourist season was a very makeshift affair, but it gave the new management some idea of what to do. A five year plan was drafted to utilize existing structures for various purposes without much renovation. Several long term plans were presented by G.S.I. people, TVA planners, private consultants, and even National Park Service planners in Washington. Several of the plans were based on the construction of the North Shore Road through the park: "When the parkway is completed along the north side of Fontana Lake between Bryson City and the dam, Fontana Village will be placed on one of the most popular tourist circuits in the southeast. For that reason all plans for the location of new facilities should give major consideration to the handling of traffic and the parking of visitor's cars." The traffic and parking congestion has never materialized—for that matter, neither has an abundance of new facilities.

Ruth J. Dallwig, recreation supervisor at Fontana, sent a lengthy proposal concerning anticipated recreational needs based on her observations and experience during Fontana's inaugural resort season to R.D. Lewis, G.S.I.'s deputy general manager, in Oc-

HOLLAND COLLECTION

**The 1950's Village.**

tober of 1946. Her report detailed dozens of recreational amenities that might help transform the former government construction village into a desirable recreation resort. Swimming pools, boating, horseback riding, concerts, movies, and water festivals were suggested, among other things. Mr. Lewis, responding from his Washington office, virtually ripped the woman apart. I guess his condescending rebuttal was a sign of the times, but I'm sure it took a bit of spark out of the 1947 recreation program.

By 1950, contract addendums had added the rest of the village property to the G.S.I. leasehold and considerable renovation had been completed to render the village into a neat, yet a bit unusual, vacation destination. The hospital was converted into a 56 room lodge, the grocery/dry goods store became the cafeteria, the drug store with its wonderful soda fountain was remodeled but retained its original function, and a new grocery store/post office building was constructed. Since 1946, Major O.A. Fetch had been the resident manager at Fontana and he would lead the property into an extended period of prosperity.

After World War II, average Americans entered an unprecedented period of self-gratification. A good job, a car, and a home of their own was finally in reach for most of the populace. Soon the idea of a vacation began to catch on. Along with Florida, the southern mountains became the preferred destinations for many families. Growing up in Atlanta in the fifties, I remember both trips. My mother gleefully told of my first trip to the ocean: after hours in the back seat of the family car we had finally reached the Sunshine State—when we stopped for a roadside break, I jumped from the car and dove into a small pond, proclaiming how great it was to be at the ocean. Although I do not exactly remember the plunge into the mud puddle or other embarrassing childhood episodes, some backed up with photographic evidence, I do remember my first trip to the mountains. The two lane highways of the day took us

**Construction era Hospital becomes tourist era Lodge.**

HOLLAND COLLECTION

HOLLAND COLLECTION

**Lodge lobby, early 1960's.**

through every small town on the seemingly endless trip from Atlanta to Gatlinburg. A simple but cozy room in a stone-veneered tourist court would be our home for the visit. Simple entertainments, scenic drives, and playing in the mountain stream outside our room embedded a lifelong love of mountains deep within me. My dad fished and my mother enjoyed someone else's cooking. These types of simple pleasures were the key to Fontana Village's early success.

Unlike Gatlinburg, Cherokee, and even Bryson City, situated on main through highways, vacationers in the 1950's that found their way to Fontana Village were probably dedicated to this destination before they left home. North Carolina Highway #28 was not constructed until the 1960's, so road access to the Village was limited to the TVA construction road that had been built from U.S.

1960's cafeteria line (above). Village shopping center in the early 1960's (below).

Highway #129 at Deals Gap. But an aggressive promotional campaign by Village management encouraged tens of thousands of tourists to make the journey. The 1952 Collins' Travelbook of North Carolina described the property as follows: "Fontana Village is a complete town for tourists on the southern edge of the Great Smoky Mountains. This unique year-round resort lies at the end of a paved highway along the Little Tennessee River, 12 miles of scenic beauty." The booklet lists all the amenities, concluding with "and other interests of civic and operational attraction." The list of recreational activities indicates that Ms. Dallwig, recreation supervisor, got most of her wishes, except the swimming pool. Rates ranged from a high of $8.00 per night for a two bedroom cottage with cooking facilities to $1.50 per night for a dormitory room. Rates were greatly reduced for longer stays and many guests spent a month or even the entire summer.

To keep everyone informed of the activities at the Village, management published the *Fontana Village News*. This weekly paper, distributed to Village guests and more importantly, mailed to prospective customers, painted an alluring picture of life at Fontana. Many issues had photos such as bathing suit clad young women cavorting in a riotous mountain steam, with a headline reading "Gals May Come, and Gals may Go—But I Flow On Forever." Then the accompanying article would quote verse from Lord Tennyson. Continuing the culture, a blurb reads "Sixteen year old Bobby Glenn Edge, who has astonished everyone with his marvelous ability as a pianist, is receiving complements at Fontana Village from guests representing many states, some of them critics of recognized competence." Of course, there were the obligatory photos of sportsmen holding

*"Gals May Come, and Gals May Go...But I Flow on Forever."*

large dead fish. Special events such as a performance of the Flying Boatmen, a group of 13 identical aluminum outboards, amazed the crowd gathered on the Dam with formations called "Snake Dance," "Three Boat Spin," and "Bombs Away" were also chronicled with text and photographs. Square Dance festivals filled the place in the off season and everyone was prosperous and happy for about 25 years.

During this period, seasoned Smoky Mountain sportsmen such as Jim Gasque, author of *Hunting and Fishing in the Great Smokies,* and other members of the old Hazel Creek Club made Fontana Village their base of operations and started to spread the word about this ready-made oasis in the center of the best outdoor sporting grounds in the east. Only a couple of years after Fontana Lake was filled, it supported a tremendous population of game fish. Gasque reported that fishermen actually complained "too many fish and too little fishing, and after fishing Fontana for several days taking limit catches each day, they sought waters that would be tougher to solve." Of course, the abundance of world class trout streams in the area provided diversion for the lake fisherman weary of dragging bass into the boat.

***Two kid fish carry.***

Arthur Stupka, the famous chief naturalist for the Great Smoky Mountains National Park, presented regularly scheduled programs and led nature hikes for Village guests. His work led to the annual Spring Flower Hike Weeks and Fall Color Hike Weeks—the year 2001 marks the 29th consecutive year these events have been held.

Fontana Village became a leader in the environmental movement even before the term became fashionable. Nationally known journalist, Garth Cate, published an article in 1960 entitled *Conser-*

HOLLAND COLLECTION

***A successful sportswoman in 1948.***

vation—American Resorts Are Dependant On It But Few Shoulder Needed Responsibility. Fontana Village resident manager, O.A. Fetch, decided to shoulder his share and with Mr. Cate's help organized the first annual Fontana Conservation Roundup. Officials from conservation and wildlife commissions were invited to the inaugural meeting. The resulting statements and policies caused such a stir that by the third Roundup, the secretaries of the Department of Interior and the Department of Agriculture were joined by the governors of eight southern states for the annual meeting. Policies proposed and adopted at these gatherings have influenced environmental decision makers ever since. Finally, after over twenty years of ground breaking work, political infighting between some of the leaders of the group resulted in them packing their toys and going home and the end of the Fontana Conservation Roundup.

The 1970's brought sobering revelations to Fontana Village

*Square dancer plays "hump the cup." The object of the game was to swing the brush suspended from their belt back and forth to knock the cup across the floor.*

management. The old worker's cabins that had served so well as tourist accommodations were now old and worn. Televisions and telephones had become standard equipment in motels and hotels everywhere. And more importantly, most people didn't take month long vacations anymore during which they got to know their fellow travellers and all the hidden treasures of their destination. Even though it wasn't quite as popular anymore, Fontana Village still retained a strong, dedicated, and vocal guest base that had enjoyed the simple pleasures of a mountain vacation for many years. They wanted nothing to do with the glitz across the mountain in Gatlinburg and Pigeon Forge with its new theme park Dollywood. But there were not enough of these long time guests to support the operation of the Village. A handful of cottages were renovated and maintenance efforts were stepped up. But the big boys at G.S.I. in Washington came up with a grand plan to modernize the Village and bring back prosperity—build a grand hotel.

Fontana Inn, completed in 1976, boasted 78 modern guest rooms with televisions and telephones (the TV only received one channel), a fine restaurant, and meeting rooms designed to attract business and other organizations meetings. Even though the Inn became popular with many guests and has hosted hundreds of group meetings, it did not succeed as the panacea for all the Village problems. In 1979, my wife and I took what we thought was a summer job at Fontana Village. We had been on a several-years journey around North America, working here and there while enjoying the sights. The area crept up on us slowly—it was two years before I completely unpacked the truck. Later we bought some land, built a house, and have been in the area ever since.

In preparation for the throngs that were expected for the 1982 World's Fair in nearby Knoxville, Tennessee, the Village Center received major renovation. The old drug store complex was torn down and the Village store building was completely remodeled, the recreation hall/registration building was renovated, and a world class miniature golf course was constructed. The World's Fair was fun but did not attract the millions of visitors that were anticipated. The new president of G.S.I. who had initiated the latest renovations, changed the name of the company to Guest Services Incorporated, and stated that Guest Services was to become the number one property management company in the country. The first step was to make a bid to take over all the visitor services at Yellowstone National Park. The times were heady around the Village—the place was in pretty good shape, business was steady, and several of us were prepared to go to Yellowstone to take over that operation. Then the bids were opened for the Yellowstone Management Contract and G.S.I. was not the winner. It was almost like—well, if we can't have Yellowstone, we just won't do property management. Within a month, Guest Services Inc. bought a national chain of pizza

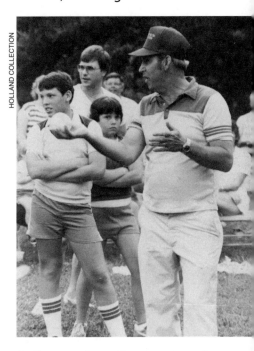

*In the evenings, the guests and employees gathered on the ballfield, chose up sides, and played for blood.*

**And at night, there were big square dances.**

stores and put the management lease at Fontana up for sale.

This was not a good thing for the people who lived and worked at Fontana Village—the possibility of losing your job was one thing, but losing your house presented serious concern. A new group of upper management was sent to Fontana whose sole agenda was to keep a lid on the place until it could be sold. This new group was commanded by general manager, Charles Munyon. As time passed, we felt like salmon at the fish market. Group after group of prospective buyers were trooped through the Village. Munyon kept everyone on a need to know basis, but it was pretty easy to tell when we were being shopped—car loads of people in suits were a little unusual at a mountain resort. Evidently,

Guest Services had a harder time than TVA did in finding someone to take over the contractual responsibilities of maintaining a small town.

After a couple of years of limbo, it all became sort of a game to those of us who stuck it out and still worked there. Then in late 1985, Mr. Munyon went off on one of his frequent trips to Washington. While he was gone, several of us were sitting around the maintenance department during a well deserved break discussing the usual—what do you know about the latest rumor of our future? I said, "I know, I'll call the TVA Citizen Action Line and ask them." I dialed the toll-free number on a speaker phone so that all the bystanders could hear and simply asked what they knew about the future of Fontana Village. The attendant taking the call asked me to hold while he connected me to someone who could help. Next I talked to a middle manager who was familiar with the situation and seemed concerned that Village employees were so ill informed. Then he asked the BIG question—"may I have your name?" When those words came out of the speakerphone, the room emptied like an exploding covey of quail. I decided that I was pretty tired of the whole situation and was prepared to suffer the possible repercussions of identifying myself so I told him my name. He asked me to hold for a moment. A few of my co-workers started creeping back into the room. Next, I talked to a member of TVA upper management who I actually had known for several years. He said that he really did not know what the current situation was but would check into it and get back to me. When I hung up the phone, everyone in the room knew that I was probably toast. Sure enough, that afternoon Munyon called down from Washington and left word that he was on his way back and wanted to see me as soon as he arrived.

The next day was a Saturday and my wife, baby daughter, and I were planning to go to Knoxville to pick up a new car we had ordered. We decided it would be prudent to wait until after the meeting with Munyon to see if there would be a change in our employment status. Around noon I stood in the parking lot at the post office when Munyon drove into the Village. He saw me and pulled into the parking lot. I could tell when he got out of the car that he was not a happy camper. He lit into me about what a stir my call had made at the home office and how embarrassing it had been for him. But he finally said "I guess you've got a right to call

***Fontana Marina at daybreak.***

the TVA Citizen Action Line, but not on my dime." I responded, "But Mr. Munyon, it was a toll-free number." Boy, did he go bad then. Evidently, I was held in pretty high regard at the home office and could not be fired for this incident. So after the reaming, my little family headed to Knoxville and picked up the new car.

In August of 1987, C. Wayne Kinser, owner of Asheville based Peppertree Resorts, rode into town to save the day. An avid outdoorsman, he had been a fan of the Fontana area for many years. He bought the management lease and embarked on a 10-year $10 million renovation of the historic property. Now it was the Village of six lives.

Many renovations were made to the property, including the construction of dozens of new two bedroom, two bath cottages. The new accommodations have whirlpools, fireplaces, modern kitchens, telephones, and televisions. A cable TV system was installed so that more than one channel was now available. A new marina with a stable of new rental boats was placed into operation. Over the years, other improvements followed including a new horse rental facility. Continuing the tradition of outdoor adventure, The Fontana Adventure Center was established in 1997. The Adventure Center houses a complete backcountry outfitters store. Camping and hiking gear is also for rent here. The mountain bike shop repairs all brands of bikes and rents full suspension mountain bikes. Fontana Village is fast becoming one of the favorite venues for mountain bike racers and spectators alike. The abundance of old railroad grades, single track trails, and logging roads that run through the Village and the surrounding forest land allow for various cross country race course configurations. The start/finish area located on the ballfield in the center of the Village is surrounded by restaurants, shops and lodgings, making Fontana one of the most user friendly race venues in the country. The Adventure Center also operates a shuttle service into the Village for the hundreds of thru-hikers on the nearby Appalachian Trail.

Wayne Kinser decided to retire in the late 1990's, and began selling his business interests. At this writing, the management lease for Fontana Village is once again for sale. We will have to wait and see what the 7th life will bring.

*Chapter 14*

# Appalachian Crossroad

The Fontana area, like all of the southern mountains, has been embracing change from time immemorial. Geologic modifications have occurred for millions of years. The first humans that arrived in the region almost immediately started messing with the natural order. They killed animals for food, built shelters, piled stones, and set fire to the forest. Change, therefore, must be a natural event. When the first Europeans arrived, the process certainly accelerated. All the changes that have effected the landscape have been as steady as time. In the 20th century, certain groups directed much of the change. Resource developers harvested and harnessed the region for personal and communal gain. Simultaneously, resource protectors worked to mitigate the effects of the developers. Both groups had good points and bad points. Without the developers, I wouldn't be writing this book in my nice warm house—and you wouldn't be reading it in yours. Without the protectors, there wouldn't be much left to write about. Like all those who have preceded us, we have decisions to make about the future.

Frankly, I think the region is in better shape now than it was 50 or even 80 years ago. Comparing old maps, photographs, and other evidence from years ago to those of today, reveals that the land is far more forested, the rivers are cleaner, and almost everyone believes that protection of the environment is essential to our continued habitation of the area. The question now is where the

**Man and Dam at night.**

line should be drawn between development and preservation.

The day of wholesale extraction of natural resources has passsed, even though the region is still rich in those resources. Private timber companies have always done a better job of producing lumber than the U.S. Forest Service because selling forest products is the primary objective of the private companies. Multiple use is the mandate for the administration of Forest Service lands. If you are a public lands manager and everyone is mad at you, you are probably doing just about right, you're not playing any favorites. It is interesting to note that there are not many large timber companies currently operating in the higher mountains of the southern Appalachians. Unlike the foothills and the Piedmont, areas that respond well to modern tree farming techniques, the mountains are just not cost effective. If people are going to live in wooden houses and read books, the bottom line is, someone has to cut down trees. The question then, is how and where is the best way and place to do it? Regardless of environmental and aesthetic concerns, the forests of the southern mountains are probably worth more to the local economy today, if left largely intact, so that tourists will visit the area and spend money to look at them.

The Fontana area boasted one of the largest mineral developments in western North Carolina in the Fontana Copper Mine. The region around Spruce Pine, North Carolina still supports a considerable mining industry. The primary natural resource extracted from the southern mountains nowadays is rock. Most of the production goes toward gravel and sand for road construction. Seems like the old nemesis of transportation has not yet been satisfactorily conquered. Coal was, and still is, an important natural resource of the southern mountains. The areas that were either blessed or cursed with coal continue to grapple with the problems associated with its extraction and processing.

Major public works had a relatively short lifespan in the United States. Unlike the Pyramids or the Great Wall of China, that took hundreds or thousands of years to complete, Americans built their big stuff really quickly. Most massive dams, lakes, waterways, industrial plants, and skyscrapers were built between 1900 and 1960. The exception to this is roads and sports stadiums. Somehow, "let's go and play" has become very important lately. A number of the large hydro-electric dams in the southern mountains are presently facing relicensing by the Federal Energy Regulatory Commission. Part of the process is to solicit public comment. Some respondents have suggested that certain dams be removed to allow a natural flow in the river channels. Since one of the major environmental challenges facing the Appalachians today is air pollution from coal-fired power plants and hydro-electricity is one of the cleanest sources of electric power, we should be careful with that alternative.

Santeetlah Dam near Robbinsville is owned and operated by Alcoa, Inc. The power from this dam goes to their aluminum plant in east Tennessee. The design of Santeetlah incorporated the use of a hydro-flume, a combination pipe and tunnel that carries the water from the dam five miles across the mountains to the power house on Cheoah reservoir. This arrangement tripled the amount of electricity that can be produced from the same amount of water. The other effect this reroute had was that a 12 mile section of the Cheoah River was de-watered except for small side streams entering the river bed. As part of the relicensing process, test

*Boating on the Cheoah River may be a part of the future.*

releases of water were made into the dry river bed from Santeetlah Dam in the summer of 2000 to determine the potential for whitewater sports and fishing. I talked to several of the paddlers that rafted or kayaked the river during the test. Unanimously, they said at the higher water flow rates, the Cheoah would be the best whitewater river in the eastern U.S. for experienced paddlers. If periodic recreational water releases into the river bed are made part of the new license, it is most likely that a substantial whitewater industry would grow around the river. On the other hand, the fishermen liked the lower water flow rates for their sport.

The population of most of the Fontana area was removed during the early 1940's and has not increased much since, because most of the land is now owned by the Federal Government. Most of the area, especially the North Shore, has regained its "Back of Beyond" status. But the population of the rest of the southern mountains has been steadily increasing and even booming in some areas since around 1970. This increase can be attributed to several factors. The "back to nature" movement popularized in the 70's encouraged many young folks to move to the mountains and make their way as best they could. The availability of outdoor sports like hiking, whitewater sports, and mountain biking attracted others. Not many younger people come to the mountains to find a high paying job. In fact, many young people native to the region leave if a high paying job is their priority.

Tourism has been the catalyst that probably produces the most population growth. People visit the region, like it here, and decide this would be a great place to retire. Americans are retiring or semi-retiring at an earlier age. Improvements in infrastructure, services, health care, and roads have made the southern mountains more attractive. Steep mountain side land that 30 years ago was not very valuable is now being carved into home sites and sold for considerable sums.

One aspect of this influx that has always amused me are the folks that want to be the last ones. They want to move in and shut the door behind them. They become vocal about planning and preservation, some even use the Z-word, zoning. Reminds me of a sign I saw while driving from California into Oregon on a back road: YOU'RE WELCOME TO VISIT OREGON BUT PLEASE GO HOME WHEN YOU'RE FINISHED. I wondered if the same sign was at the Washington border or just directed at the Californians.

The Southern Appalachian Assessment—a recent, wide ranging study on the region's forests and surrounding environment—stated that "fast growth and development in the southern Appalachians are changing forever the character of the landscape." Based on the removal of man-made development in the Fontana area, I'm not sure I agree with the "forever" part of that statement. A couple of years of extreme drought, a couple of really big fires—and many of the new homes being built on steep mountain sides might not be very permanent.

The report further states: "Poverty in the region has declined dramatically in the past two decades, and the economy is changing. For example, 30 percent of the personal income in the region now comes from non-labor sources, such as retirement or investment income." That's great, but the other 70% has to make a living somehow. The Assessment compares itself to a similar study of the region in 1902, the Roosevelt Report. It will be interesting to see if the backfire effect repeats itself.

While their relative importance is changing, traditional eco-

HOLLAND COLLECTION

nomic engines such as logging, agriculture, and manufacturing are presently being joined by construction, services, health care, and tourism to create a diverse economic picture. Tourism has become the largest industry in western North Carolina and appears to continue to grow. This trend is occurring all over the southern mountains. Hopefully, a clear understanding of all the forces of change, and appropriate action by regional leaders and decision makers will render the southern Appalachian mountains a good place to live and work or just visit for many years to come. A good understanding of the past is often helpful in planning for the future.

The future of the people of the Fontana area, western North Carolina, and the southern Appalachians as a whole can be summed up by an old mountain story. A traveler from a far away city encountered an old mountain dweller alongside a dusty back road. They struck up a conversation, with the city fellow doing most of the talking.

"Well, have you lived here all your life?" he asked just before departing.

"Not yet," the old man replied.

# Sources of Information

This section is for readers who would like to learn more about a specific topic, the Fontana area in general, or the southern Appalacians as a whole. Most history writers either choose or are assigned a topic, research the selected subject, and then write their book. *Fontana—A Pocket History of Appalachia* sort of just evolved. Soon after I arrived in the Fontana area in 1979, I became fascinated with the unique history of the place. Over the years of relating this history in verbal form during the thousands of hikes, talks, and demonstrations I have led or presented—participants would often say:"you should write a book about this." So finally, I did.

A combination of books, papers, interviews, maps, and field research were all utilized in collecting this information. Following is the list of sources used.

### Books

Adams, Paul J., *Mt. LeConte*, Holston Printing Company, 1966.
Alexander, Tom, *Mountain Fever*, Alexander, 1995.
Appalachian Land Ownership Task Force, *Appalachian Land Ownership Study*, 1980.
Arthur, John P., *Western North Carolina, A History*, E.H.D. Morrison, 1914.
Badger, Anthony, *North Carolina and the New Deal*, North Carolina Division of Archives and History, 1981.
Bartram, William, *Travels of William Bartram*, Macy-Masius, 1928.
Bisher, Catherine, *A Guide To The Historic Architecture Of Western North Carolina*, UNC, Press, 1999.

Blethen, Tyler, and Wood, Curtis, *From Ulster to Carolina*, WCU 1983.
Boyden, Lucille, *The Village of Five Lives*, G.S.I., 1964.
Brewer, Alberta and Carson, *Valley So Wild: A Folk History*, E.T.H.S. 1975.
Brewer, Carson, *The Great Smokies*, Tenpenny, 1981.
Campbell, Carlos, *Birth of a National Park in the Great Smoky Mountains*, University of Tennessee Press, 1960.
Carley, Rachel, *A Guide To Biltmore Estate*, Biltmore Company, 1995.
Carr, Charles C., *Alcoa—An American Enterprise*, Rinehart & Co., 1952.
Cohen, Stan, *The Tree Army*, Pictorial Histories Publishing Co., 1980.
Daniels, Karen, *Tennessee's Historic Copper Basin Area: An Overview*, Polk County, 1992.
Dargan, Olive, *From My Highest Hill*, Scribners, 1925.
Duffus, R.L., *The Valley And It's People*, A. Knopf, 1946.
Dunn, Durwood, *Cades Cove*, U.T. Press, 1988.
Dykeman, Wilma, and Stokely, Jim, *Highland Homeland, The People of the Great Smokies*, National Park Service, 1981.
Ehle, John, *Trail of Tears*, Anchor, 1988.
Forest, G., *Great Adventures in the Southern Appalachians*, John F. Blair, 1994.
Frome, Michael, *Strangers In High Places*, University of Tennessee Press, 1966.
Gasque, Jim, *Hunting and Fishing in the Great Smokies*, Knopf, 1948.
George, Michael, *Southern Railways Murphy Branch*, The College Press, 1996.
Harshaw, Lou, *Asheville*, Harshaw, 1980.
Housley, J. Elmer, *Tapoco's Hydroelectric Developments in the Smoky Mountains*, Tapoco, INC., 1957.
Johnson, Bruce, *A History of the Grove Park Inn*, Grove Park, 1991.
Johnson, C. and Jackson, C., *City Behind A Fence, Oak Ridge, Tennessee*, University of Tennessee Press, 1981.
Kephart, Horace, *Camping and Woodcraft*, MacMillan, 1917.
Kephart, Horace, *Our Southern Highlanders*, MacMillan, 1913.
Kephart, Horace, *The Cherokees of the Smoky Mountains*, Kephart, 1936.
King, Duane, and Evans, Raymond, *Journal of Cherokee Studies, Volume IV, No. 4*, Museum of the Cherokee Indian, 1979.
Koch, Michael, *Steam & Thunder In The Timber*.
Lanman, Charles, *Letters From The Allegheny Mountains*, 1849.
Lilienthal, David, *TVA—Democracy On The March*, Pocket Books, 1944.
Lowe, Mary Jane, *Voices In The Valley*, TVA, 1993.
Mastran, Shelley, and Lowerre, Nan, *Mountaineers And Rangers*, U.S. Forest Service, 1983.
McRae, Barbara, *Franklin's Ancient Mound*, Teresita Press, 1993.
Middleton, Harry, *On The Spine Of Time*, Simon & Schuster, 1991.

Mooney, James, *Myths of the Cherokee and Sacred Formulas of the Cherokees*, Elder, 1982.
*Nantahala Power and Light Hydroelectric Projects FERC Relicensing Handbook*, NP&L, 1999.
National Park Service, *At Home In The Smokies*, NPS, 1984.
Oakley, Wiley, *Roamin & Restin*, Oakley, 1940.
Oliver, Duane, *Along the River: People and Places*, Oliver, 1998.
Oliver, Duane, *Hazel Creek From Then Til Now*, Oliver, 1989.
Oliver, Duane, *Remembered Lives: A Narrative History*, Oliver, 1993.
Parce, Meade, *Railroad Through The Back Of Beyond*, Harmon Den Press, 1997.
Parris, John, *Roaming The Mountains*, Citizen-Times, 1955.
Perdue, Theda, *The Cherokee*, Chelsea, 1989.
Pinchot, Gifford, *Breaking New Ground*.
Reed, Oren, *Fontana Dam Construction*, TVA, 1946.
Robinson, Blackwell, *North Carolina Guide*, UNC, Press, 1955.
Rozema, Vicki, *Footsteps of the Cherokees*, Blair, 1995.
Schenck, Carl, *Birth of Forestry in America*, Appalachian Consortium, 1955.
Schmidt, Rondald and Hooks, William, *Whistle Over The Mountain*, Graphicom Press, 1994.
Shands, William, and Healy, Robert, *The Lands That Nobody Wanted*, The Conservation Foundation, 1977.
Sheppard, Muriel, *Cabins In The Laurel*, UNC, Press, 1935.
Steen, Harold, *The U.S. Forest Service A History*, University of Washington Press, 1976.
Stupka, Arthur, *Great Smoky Mountains National Park*, N.P.S., 1960.
Thornborough, Laura, *The Great Smoky Mountains*, University of Tennessee Press, 1937.
Trotter, William, *Bushwhackers*, Blair, 1958.
TVA, *Construction and Maintenance Division, Final Cost Report, Fontana. Access Road Camp and Village, Fontana Dam*, TVA, 1945.
TVA, *Fontana Project Final Construction Report*, Five Volumes, 1946.
TVA, *The First Fifty Years: Changed Land, Changed Lives*, TVA, 1983.
TVA, *The Fontana Project*, TVA, 1950.
TVA, *The Tennessee River Navigation System*, TVA, 1964.
TVA, *Surveying, Mapping, and Related Engineering*, TVA, 1951.
Weals, Vic, *Last Train To Elkmont*, Olden Press, 1991.
Wigginton, Eliot, *Foxfire*, Anchor Books, 1986.
Woodward, Grace, *The Cherokees*, Univ. of Oklahoma, 1963.
York, Thomas, *America's Great Railroads*, Bison Books Ltd., 1987.
Various, *Bryson City Centennial Book*, Bryson City, NC, 1989.
Various, *Graham County Centennial Book*, Graham County, 1972.

Various, *Report on the Forests and Forest Conditions of the Southern Appalachian Mountain Region*, U.S. Department of Agriculture, 1902.
Zeigler, Wilbur, and Grosscup, Ben, *The Heart of the Alleghanies*, Williams, 1883.

## Papers

Agreement between J.C. Gunter and J.F. Loomis and Xebaphon Wheeler, Graham County, NC, Deed Book, 1885.
Agreement between J.C. Gunter and W.C. Heyser & Co., Graham County, NC, Deed Book, 1891.
Alexander, James W., *Letter to C.H. McNaughton*, 1944.
Alexander, James W., *Letter to Dr. W.H. Emmons*, 1943.
Asheville Radio Station WWNC, Script, *Fontana Goes To War*, May 20, 1943.
Cashion, Jerry, *Fort Butler and the Cherokee Indian Removal From North Carolina*, State Department of Archives and History, 1970.
Cate, Garth, *Conservation—American Resorts Are Dependant On It But Few Shoulder Needed Responsibility*, 1960.
Cities Services, Fontana Mine Assays, 1931–1942.
Columbia Broadcasting System Script, *Transatlantic Call, People To People, No. 45—Dreamers With Shovels*, Sunday, Dec. 12, 1943.
Couch, R.H., TVA Cafeteria Manager, Scrapbook, 1945.
Ellison, George, Chronology, *1943 Agreement Controversy*, 1992.
Ellison, Quinten, and Wall, Sandy, *Despite New Funding, 'Road To Nowhere's' Future Still In Doubt*, Asheville Citizen-Times, Nov. 27, 2000.
Emmons, W.H., *A Report on the Fontana Mine*, 1942.
Ferguson, Vernon V., *Some Memories of the Fontana Coppermine Era*, Fontana North Shore Historical Association Newsletter, 1993.
Graham County, NC, Deedbooks, Robbinsville, NC.
Hyde, Arnold, *Stecoah Community, Fontana Area*, TVA Property Management Population Readjustments, 1944.
Hyde, B.F., *Cities Services Interoffice Memo to M.F. Finfrock*, 1975.
Kendall, H.F., *Some Copper-zinc Bearing Pyrrhotite Ore Bodies In Tennessee and North Carolina*, 1950.
Kephart, Horace, *A National Park In The Great Smoky Mountains*, Swain County Chamber of Commerce, 1926.
Ketchen, F.E., *Bushnell Community Study, Fontana Area*, TVA Property Management Population Readjustment, 1944.
*Logging and Lumbering Operations in the Smoky Mountains*, National Park Service, Gatlinburg, Tennessee.
Loney, Jon M., *The Ocoee River Controversy—Arriving at a Solution*, TVA, 1984.
McDaniel, Edgar L., Jr., *Letters To National Park Service*, 1953.

Mynders, Alfred, *Next To The News*, Chattanooga Times, Sept. 1944.
O'Brien, Robert D., *National Park Service Report: Evaluation of the Fontana Mine*, 1972.
Paxton, Percy J., *National Forests and Purchase Units of Region Eight*, United States Forest Service, 1950.
Rockefeller Agreement, *The Laura Spelman Rockefeller Memorial*, 1928.
Sandford, Jason, *Neill, Environmentalists, Blast Taylor's Effort On Behalf Of Road*, Asheville Citizen-Times, Nov. 2000.
Sharp, Rome, *Proctor Community, Fontana*, TVA Property Management Population Readjustments, 1944.
Schlemmer, Fred, Various Letters, Reports, and Statements, 1942–1945.
Stewart, Phillip O., *National Park Service Memorandum to Director, Southeast Region*, 1972.

**Interviews and Contributions**

Fred Alexander, District Manager, Nantahala Power & Light Company, a division of Duke Power Company, Franklin, NC, 1999.
Bob Allman, Public Relations Director, Norfolk-Southern Railway, 1999.
Sheila Beasley, former Fontana Dam, NC, Postmaster, 1986–1995.
Eloise Barton Brock, Dam Kid, 1994.
Violet Briggs, Personnel Manager, Fontana Village, 1988–2001.
Walter Brosnan, grandson of Bill Brosnan, former President of Southern Railway, 2000.
Linda Cable, Swain County Administrator, Bryson City, NC, 1999, 2000.
Kathryne Caine, Jessie Gunter's granddaughter, 1989.
Gay Calhoun, son of Fontana miner, 1990.
Wallace Calhoun, son of Fontana miner, Bryson City, NC, 1990.
Leonard Carpenter, former Fontana Village employee, Robbinsville, NC, 1980–1990.
Lester Carringer, Fontana Marina Manager, 1996, 1999, 2001.
Jim Casada, author and educator, Rock Hill, SC, 2001.
Dorothy Barton Chewning, Dam Kid, 1994.
Doris Couch Clayton, Dam Kid, 1986, 1991, 1997, 1999.
Shirley Crisp, Stecoah, NC, 1995.
Dozens of Dam Kids, 1986–1999.
Dozens of former and current Fontana Village employees, 1979–2001.
Dozens of former North Shore residents, 1982–2001.
George Ellison, historian and author of introduction to *Our Southern Highlanders* by Horace Kephart and *Myths of the Cherokee* by James Mooney, Bryson City, NC, 1990–2001.
Frank Finley, Asst. Ranger, Cheoah Ranger District, U.S. Forest Service, 1997, 1998, 1999.

George Frizzell, Head of Special Collections, Hunter Library, Western Carolina University, 1985–2001.
Tommy and Marie Gladden, former North Shore residents, Robbinsville, NC, 1989, 1994.
Burlin Green, historian and son of Kitchens Lumber Company employee, Robbinsville, NC, 1991.
Annette Hartigan, Librarian, Great Smoky Mountains National Park, 2001.
Barry Hipps, General Manager, Cherokee Historical Association, 2001.
Billy Holder, grading contractor, Robbinsville, NC, 1999.
Ray Johns, Lands Program Manager, U.S. Forest Service, 1999.
Mildred Cable Johnson, former North Shore Resident, Andrews, NC, 1992.
Robert Johnson, antique machineries expert, Rossville, Georgia, 1988, 1990.
David Kerr, General Manager, Fontana Village, NC, 2000.
C. Wayne Kinser, Owner, Fontana Village Management Lease, 2001.
John R. Kitchen, son of Kitchen Lumber Company founder, Ashland, KY, 1989.
Gene and Carrie Laney, former North Shore residents, Robbinsville, NC, 1988, 1995, 1997, 1999.
Jimmy Marsh, Dam Kid, 1994.
Bob Miller, Management Assistant, Great Smoky Mountains National Park, 1995, 1998, 2001.
Pat Momich, Interpretative Specialist, U.S. Forest Service, 1999.
Blanche Noble, Jessie Gunter's granddaughter, 1989.
Danny Olinger, Archeologist, TVA, 1990.
Duane Oliver, historian, author, and former North Shore resident, 1999, 2000, 2001.
Mike O'Neal, railroad historian, Tullahoma, Tennessee, 1989.
Mead Parce, author, 2001.
Henry and Alice Posey, former North Shore residents, Franklin, NC, 1988.
Tom Robbins, Park Ranger, Great Smoky Mountains National Park, 1995, 1999.
Simme Roten, manuscript reader, Robbinsville, NC, 2001.
Ken Rush, Director, Ducktown Basin Museum, 1989, 1990, 1996, 1999, 2001.
Rodney Schnidecker, Archeologist, U.S. Forest Service, 1998.
Nelson Seaman, Dam Kid, 1985, 1990, 1995, 2000.
Beverly Smythy, Jessie Gunter's great-granddaughter, 1989.
Jeannie Stewart, manuscript reader, Whittier, NC, 2001.
Charles Tichy, Historic Architect, TVA, 1986, 1990, 1994, 1999.
Ed Trout, Park Historian, Great Smoky Mountains National Park, 1989, 1993.
Willa Mae Trull, former North Shore resident, Balsam, NC, 1986, 1990.

Luther Turpin, Fontana Marina Manager (ret.) Fontana, NC, 1979–2001.
Helen Cable Vance, former North Shore resident, Sylva, NC, 1982–2001.
Harvey Welch, Dam Kid, 1985, 1990.
Bob Wightman, Staff Park Ranger, Great Smoky Mountains National Park, 2001.

**Maps**

Holland, Lance, map of Fontana Copper Mine Camp, 1990.
Holland, Lance, map of Proctor, NC, 1988.
Kephart, Horace, map of Hazel Creek, 1906.
Mac Rae, John, State of North Carolina, 1833.
National Park Service, Great Smoky Mountains National Park Boundary Analysis (showing Cammerer Line), 1977.
North Carolina, Post Route Map, 1896.
TVA, Fontana Dam Site and Vicinity (pre-construction), 1941.
TVA, Fontana Dam Site Topography, TVA, 1944.
TVA, Land Acquisition Maps, Fontana Reservoir, 19-MS-421 K504–sheets 1 through 39, TVA, 1942.
USGS, Planemetric Advance Sheets for TVA, Fontana, Proctor, Judson, and Wesser Quads, 1936.
USGS, Proposed Great Smoky Mountains National Park, 1929.
USGS Topographic Maps, USGS, various.

**Periodicals**

*Fontana Village News*, 1951–1995.
*Hardwood Bark*, W.M. Ritter Lumber Company Newsletter, Columbus, Ohio, 1922–1929.
*The Southern Lumberman*, Kitchen Lumber Company To Develop Lumber Holdings Near Fontana, NC, 1920.
*Fontana North Shore Historical Association Newsletter*, 1986–2001.

**Catalogs**

*The Lima Locomotive Company*, Lima, Ohio.
*The Climax Patent Geared Locomotives, Catalog K*, 1917.

**Videos**

*Construction of Fontana Dam*, TVA, 1947.
*Hiking on Hazel Creek*, Producer Lance Holland, Appalachian History Series, 1993.

## 234 Fontana: A Pocket History of Appalachia

*Nantahala...Land of the Noonday Sun*, Producers, Lance Holland, George Ellison, Ron Ruehl, Appalachian History Series, 1998.
*Road To Nowhere*, Producers Jim Bramblet, Robin Briggs, UNC, Public Television, 1997.
*Seasons in the Smokies*, Producer, Tom Alexander, Cataloochee Ranch, 1950.
*The Tennessee Valley Authority*, Modern Marvels, The History Channel, 1998.

# Index

### A

Adair, James, 11
Adams, Paul J., 113
Adams, W.S., 46, 196
Adams-Westfeldt Copper Mine, 47, 50, 202
AGREEMENT, 1943, 187
Alarka Lumber Company, 79
Alexander, J.W., 52, 56
Almond Boat Dock, 14
Almond School, 103
Aluminum Company of America (Alcoa), 86, 121, 123, 132, 136, 173, 181, 223
Ambler, Chase P., 109, 113
American Hoist and Derrick Company, 87
Amherst, Jeffery, 27
Anakeesta Formation, 191
Ancih, 19
Andrews, North Carolina, 15, 76
Andrus, Cecil, 195
Anthony, Luther, 88
Appalachian Mountain Club, 65
Appalachian National Park Association, 65, 109
Appalachian Power Company, 134
Arthur, Gabriel, 23
Ashe, C.C. and Pearl, 186
Asi, 12
Attakullakulla, 9, 27, 28
Auroria, Georgia, 13
Ayers, R.R., 206

### B

Babcock Boom & Lumber Company, 61
Baldwin Locomotive Works, 81
Bartram Society, 27
Bartram, William, 11, 27, 28
Battle of Horseshoe Bend, 13
Berger, J., 91
Big Bear's place, 15
Big Junaluska, 88
Biltmore Estate, 105, 109, 201
Blue Ridge Railroad, 72
Bone Valley, 96
Bone Valley Cemetery, 105
Bone Valley Creek, 46
Boudinot, Elias, 14
Bowmaster, Wylie, 132
Boyden, Lucile K., 134, 202
Bradley, Isaac, 34
Bradshaw, J.W., 96
Brendle, Pearly, 102
Brewer, Alberta and Carson, 88, 123, 134
Brock, Eloise Barton, 155
Brooks, Lillie Lucille, 105
Bryson City, North Carolina, 15, 45, 75
Bryson, Mark, 46
Buchanon Lumber Company, 79
Burke McDowell Lumber Company, 110
Burlingame, Orson P., 105
Burnett, Louada, 102
Bushnell, NC, 15, 47, 75, 80, 128, 183

## C

Cable, Linda, 196
Cable, Samuel and Elizabeth, 37
Cades Cove, TN, 34
Calderwood, 123
Calderwood Dam, 124
Calderwood, I.G., 123
Caldwell, Dr. John, 71
Calhoun, Gay, 190
Calhoun, Granville, 48, 98
Calhoun, John C., 71
Calhoun, Sanders, 106
Calhoun-Coburn School, 102
Cammerer, Arno B., 116
Cannon, Joseph G., 110
Carolina & Tennessee Southern Railroad, 54, 72, 80, 87, 183
Carolina Aluminum Company, 127
Carr, Charles C., 122
Cate, Garth, 212
Chapman, David C., 113
Charleston, North Carolina, 15
Charleston, South Carolina, 15, 24
Chattanooga, Tennessee, 14, 61
Cheoah Dam, 86, 124
Cheoah Lake, 86, 88, 125, 135
Cheoah, NC, 11
Cheoah Ranger District, 111
Cheoah River, 27, 123, 126, 223
Cherokee, North Carolina, 12
Cherokee Phoenix, 13
Chewning, Dorothy Barton, 158
Chief Junaluska, 13
Chief Oconostota, 26
Chief Yonaguska, 16
Chilhowee, Tennessee, 11, 123
Chota, 23
Cities Services Realty Corporation, 55, 57
Citizen Cherokees, 16
Civil War, 37, 73

Clapp, George H., 121
Clarke, Jamie, 195
Clarke-McNary Amendment, 110
Clayton, Doris Couch, 155
Climax Locomotives, 83
Climax Manufacturing Company, 83
Clinton, Bill, 196
Coburn, J.E., 111
Collins, Robert, 34
Conley, Polly Sherrill, 34
Cook, Bent, 46
Cooke Locomotive & Machinery, 81
Cooper, James Fenemore, 27
Cooper, Peter, 71
Copperhill, Tennessee, 49
Couch, R.H., 144
Cowee, 28, 29
Cowee Tunnel, 75
Creek Indians, 14
Cuming, Sir Alexander, 24

## D

Dallwig, Ruth J., 206
Dam Kids, 155
Danielson, Arthur, 90
Davey, Sir Humphry, 119
Davis, Arthur V., 127
Davis, Willis P., 112
De Soto, Hernando, 23
Deadening, 36
Deals Gap, 15
Debord, Lottie, 102
Ducktown Basin Museum, 55
Ducktown Chemical and Iron Company, 50
Ducktown, Tennessee, 55
Duke Power Company, 128

## E

Eagle Creek, 79, 85
Echota, Georgia, 14
Ecoah Branch, 50
Edge, Bobby Glenn, 211
Elliott, John, 25
Ellis, Vincent, 193
Ellison, George, 192

Emmons, Dr. W.H., 56
Enloe, Abraham, 34
Euchella, 19
Evans, Raymond E., 17
Everett, Ep, 46

## F

Farmstead, Pioneer Museum, 34
Federal Energy Regulatory Commission, 127, 223
Federal Power Commission, 133
Felmet, David, 195
Fetch, O.A., 208, 213
Fish traps, 12
Flying Boatmen, 212
Fontaine, Felice, 203
Fontana Adventure Center, 219
Fontana Conservation Roundup, 213
Fontana Copper Mine, 50, 56, 135, 188, 190
Fontana Mining Corporation, 50
Fontana, North Carolina, 203
Fontana North Shore Historical Association, 193
Fontana Schools, 155
Fontana Village, 42, 145, 155
Ford, Harrison, 124
Ford, Henry, 149
Forney Creek, 79
Forney, NC, 80
Fort Delaney, 15
Fort Lindsay, 14
Fort Loudon, 25
Fort Montgomery, 14
Fort Prince George, 27
Foster, William S., 19
Franklin, North Carolina, 10
Fraser, John, 30
French Broad River, 72
Frome, Michael, 113

## G

Galloway, Emma, 102
Gasque, Jim, 212

Gatlinburg, Tennessee, 201
General Eustis, 15
Georgia and North Carolina Railroad, 76
Gold, 55
Government Services Inc., 205
Governor Bull, 27
Graham County Lumber Company, 79
Grant, James, 27
Grant, Ulysses S., III, 205
Great Depression, 55
Great Smoky Mountain Railway, 184, 201
Great Smoky Mountains Conservation Association, 112
Great Smoky Mountains National Park, 9, 10, 49, 57, 116, 135, 186, 188, 192, 196, 200, 205
Green, Burlin, 135
Gregg, William C., 113
Grey, Asa, 30
Grossman, Elizabeth, 152
Grove Park Inn, 112, 113
Gudger, Lamar, 195
Guest Services Incorporated, 215
Gunter, Catherine, 34
Gunter, Cyrene, 39
Gunter Gap, 15
Gunter, Hiram and Bettie, 38
Gunter, Jessie, 34, 37, 62, 146
Gunters' Landing, 14
Gunterville, Alabama, 14

## H

H.K. Porter & Company, 81
Hall, A.E., 121
Hall, Charles Martin, 119, 120, 128
Hall, Crate, 46
Hall, Fonzie, 45
Hall, Mary, 102
Hanks, Nancy, 34
Harding, Warren G., 111
Hazel Creek, 35, 45, 48, 49, 60, 79, 81, 90

Hazel Creek Fishing and Outing Club, 202
Helms, Jesse, 195, 196
Henry, Rowe, 102
Hicks, John, 98
Hiesler Locomotive Company, 83
Highlands, North Carolina, 112
Hipps, Jimmy, 161
Hodges, Luther, 191
Holland, William Thomas, 16
Holmes, Joseph A., 109
Hoover, Herbert, 111
Horner, I.G., 102
Hyatt, R., 102
Hyde, Martin and Rachel, 97

## I

Isabella, Tennessee, 50, 55

## J

Jackson, Andrew, 13
James, John, and Charles Kitchens, 86
Joanna Bald, 15
Johnson, Mildred Cable, 193
Jolly, T.D., 121
Joyce Kilmer Memorial Forest, 11, 27
Judson, 15, 80, 91, 185

## K

Kahn, Albert, 149, 152
Kelsey, Harlan P., 113
Kephart, Horace, 64, 113, 115, 200, 201
King, Duane, 17
King George II, 25
Kinser, C. Wayne, 218
Kitchen, James H., 86, 135
Kitchen, John R., 86, 135
Kitchens, Charles, 86, 89
Kitchens Lumber Company, 79, 86, 88, 134
Kitchensville, 86, 135
Kituwha, 23

## L

Lakeshore Drive, 191
Lanman, Charles, 16
Laura Spelman Rockefeller Memorial, 115
Leatherwood, Ron, 196
LeConte Lodge, 113
Lillienthal, David, 133, 141
Lima Locomotive Company, 83
Lincoln, Abraham, 34
Little Fork Ridge, 45
Little River, 86
Little River Lumber Company, 85
Little Tennessee River, 9, 10, 60, 72, 73, 123, 128
Little Tennessee Turnpike, 15
Littlefield, Milton, 74
Log boom, 61
Long Creek, 15
Loomis & Wheeler, 59
Loomis, J.F., 62
Lowe, Mary Jane, 161
Lower Cherokees, 10

## M

Marcy, Dr. Henry O., 109
Marsh, Jimmy, 158, 161, 175
Marvel Lumber Company, 79
Maryville, Tennessee, 123
McDaniel, Edgar L., Jr., 191
McShane, Hugh, 166
Medlin, NC, 47
Meigs Creek, 86
Merritt, Clyde, 161
Michaux, Andre, 30
Middle Cherokees, 10
Miller, Bob, 196
Mingus, John, 34
Montgomery, Archibald, 26
Montvale Coronet Band, 90
Montvale Lumber Company, 50, 79, 203
Mooney, James, 12
Moore, Dan, 193
Moore, N.D., 91
Morgan, Arthur, 133, 149
Mt. LeConte, 113
Mull, Rob, 52

## Index 237

Murphy Branch, 75, 80, 183, 201
Murphy, NC, 76
Murphy, Neil, 195
Museum of the Cherokee Indian, 17
Mynders, Alfred, 162
Myths of the Cherokee, 12

## N

Nantahala National Forest, 205
Nantahala Outdoor Center, 185
Nantahala Power and Light Company, 127, 133
Nantahala River, 27, 28
Nantayalee George, 19
Nantayalee Jake, 19
Narrows, 9
National Forest Reservation Commission, 110
National Park Service, 21
Needham, James, 23
Neill, Sam, 196
Nelson, Donald M., 163
New Deal, 131
Niagara Falls Power Company, 122
Nikwasi, 10
North Carolina Exploration Company, 55, 204
North Carolina Park Commission, 115
North Shore Cemetery Association, 193
North Shore Road, 191, 192, 194, 196, 201
Northfork Southern, 75
Norwood Lumber Company, 79

## O

O'Brien, Robert D., 57
Ocoee #2 Dam, 125
Ocoee River, 125, 127
Oconaluftee, 12
Oconaluftee Indians, 16

Oconaluftee Living Indian Village, 12
Oconaluftee River, 34
Oconaluftee Visitors Center, 34
Oersted, H.C., 119
Old Fort Mountain, 74
Olinger, Danny, 185
Oliver, Duane, 91, 189
Oliver, E.H., 102
Oliver, Zina Farley, 98
Orr, Will, 88
Overhill Cherokees, 10

## P

Panther Creek, 15
Pardo, Juan, 23
Parson's Turnpike, 123
Patterson, John Lee, 179
Payne, David Lee, 179
Payne, Vate, 94
Peppertree Resorts, 218
Pinchot, Gifford, 109
Pisgah National Forest, 201
Pittsburgh Reduction Company, 121
Poinsett, Joel, 71
Post, Dr., 50
Prince, Jack, Sr., 49
Proctor Cemetery, 35, 193
Proctor, Moses and Patience, 34
Proctor School, 102
Proctor, William Crow, 38

## Q

Quallatown, 34

## R

Randolph, R.L., 102
Red Marble Gap, 76
Rhea, Wilie, 102
Richardson, Nancy Catherine, 38
Richmond and Danville Railroad Company, 76
Rickman, A.J., 91

Ridge, Major, 14
Riter, Dr. J.F., 50, 52
Ritter Lumber Company, 79, 81, 104
Ritter, NC, 100
Ritter Station, 80
Robbinsville, North Carolina, 11, 14
Rockefeller, John D., Jr., 115
Rogers, Mel, 98
Rogers, W.N., 141
Roosevelt, Franklin Delano, 116, 128, 131
Roosevelt, Theodore, 66, 69
Ross' Landing, 14
Rucker, Phil, 158
Rymers Ferry Power House, 53

## S

Santeetlah Dam, 124, 127, 223
Schlemmer, Fred, 144, 155, 162
Scott, Winfield, 14
Seaman, Nelson, 156
Sequoyah, 13
Shay, Ephraim, 83
Shay locomotives, 83
Silers Bald, 49
Silver, 55
Sluder, Joseph P., 88
Smith, A.J., 16
Smith, C.D., 109
Smoky Mountain Railroad Company, 81, 96
Soco Creek, 34
Southern Appalachian Assessment, 225
Southern Appalachian National Park Commission, 112, 114
Southern Railway Company, 77, 80, 135, 183
Splash dams, 60
Squires, Mark, 113, 115
Stecoah Gap, 15
Stecoah valley, 15
Stephenson, Robert, 71
Stewart, Phillip O., 57

Stickball, 29
Stikeleather, J.G., 202
Storie, Dr. J.G., 100
Stuart, Polly, 102
Stupka, Arthur, 212
Sugar Fork, 47
Swain County Chamber of Commerce, 115
Sweetwater Creek, 15
Swepson, George, 74

## T

Tallapoosa River, 14
Tallasee Power Company, 124
Tapoco Inc., 124, 127
Tatham Gap, 15
Tatham Gap Road, 15
Taylor & Crate, 59
Taylor, Charles, 196
Taylor, Roy, 193
Tellico River, 10
Tennessee Copper and Chemical Company, 55
Tennessee River, 14
Tennessee Valley Authority, 21, 49, 57, 119, 131
Tennyson, Lord, 211
The Fugitive, 124
The Road To Nowhere, 191
Thomas, William H., 71
Thorpe, J.E.S., 133
Tichy, Charles, 127, 152
Townsend, W.B., 85
Trail of Tears, 9
Treaty of 1819, 15, 33
Treaty of New Echota, 14
Trout, Ed, 39
Tsali, 16
Tuckasegee River, 12, 75
Twenty Mile Creek, 79, 86, 88, 135

## U

U.S. Coast Guard, 134
U.S. Forest Service, 109, 111, 188, 205, 222
Unaka mountains, 10

## V

Vance, Helen Cable, 193
Vanderbilt, George, 105
Vickers, Bob, 174
Virginia Railroad, 72
Vivian, 87, 88

## W

W.C. Heyser & Co., 59, 63
W.J. Best & Company, 75
Wachacha, 19
Wank, Roland, 148
War Production Board, 187
Wasseton, 19
Watkins, Arthur, 52, 91
Watt, Thomas, 71
Weals, Vic, 88
Weeks Act, 110
Welch Cove, 37, 155, 204
Welch Cove Cemetery, 42
Welch, Dilly, 50
Welch, Elvira, 102
Welch, Harvey, 156
Welch, J.W., 96, 101
Welch, Joe (Joseph), 15
Welch, Josiah, 38
Western North Carolina Railroad, 72
Westfeldt, George, 47, 196
Wheeler, Xebaphon, 62
Whiting Manufacturing Company, 38, 79, 111, 135
Wiggins, Maude, 102
Wilderness Act, 193
Williams, W.G., 15, 18, 33
Wilson, Charley, 91
Wilson, Grace, 102
Wilson, J.H., 91
Wilson, James, 66
Wilson, Joe, 102
Wilson, Mary, 102
Wilson, Woodrow, 110
Winston, Joseph, 14
Winston, Joseph, Chapter of the Daughters of the American Revolution, 14
Wolf Creek, 15
Wood, Abraham, 23
Wood, George and R.E., 50
Wood, Mrs. George Leidy, 203
Work, Hubert, 112
World War II, 9

## Y

Yellowstone National Park, 215